BASIC V

For the Acorn Archimedes

Mike Williams

BASIC V
For the Acorn Archimedes

Copyright © Mike Williams 1989-2014
Fourth Edition October 2014

Editor: David Bradforth
Cover: Clare Atherton
Illustrations: Ian Bishop-Laggett
Thanks to: Aaron Timbrell & Dave Holden

Within this book the letters BBC refer to the British Broadcasting Corporation. The terms BBC micro, Master 128, Master Compact and Archimedes refer to the computers manufactured by Acorn Computers Ltd under licence from the BBC. InterWord is published by Computer Concepts Ltd.

All rights reserved. No part of this book (except brief passages quoted for critical purposes) or any of the computer programs to which it relates may be reproduced or translated in any form, by any means, mechanical electronic or otherwise, without the prior written consent of the copyright holder.

Disclaimer: Because neither the author nor publisher have any control over the way in which the material in this book is used, no warranty is given, or should be implied, as to the suitability of the advice or programs for any given application. No liability can be accepted for any consequential loss or damage, however caused, arising as a result of using the programs or advice printed in this book.

Published by   David Bradforth
                16 Rodney Way
                Romford
                Essex RM7 8PD

Typeset in 10 on 11pt Palatino using Adobe InDesign

Printed and bound by Amazon CreateSpace.

ISBN-13: 978-1502862440
ISBN-10: 1502862441

BASIC V For the Acorn Archimedes

Contents

1 : Introduction	7
2 : Operators	9
New Assignment Operators	9
New Unary Operators	10
New Binary Operators	11
Swapping Variables	13
3 : String Handling	15
String Functions	15
String Handling in Files	17
Organisation and Allocation of String Storage	17
New Memory Allocation System	18
4 : Control Structures	20
WHILE Loops	20
Block-structured IF	21
The CASE statement	22
5 : Procedures & Functions	26
Passing Parameters	26
Passing Arrays as Parameters	38
Local Arrays	29
Procedure and Function Libraries	30
Dynamic Loading of Procedure	32
6 : Error Handling	33
Local Error Trapping	33
Local DATA	37
New ERROR Keyword Usage	38
Revised Error Numbers and Messages	38
7 : Matrices	40
Introducing Whole-Array Operations	41
Whole-Array Operations: Constants	42
Arrays: Operation on with a Constant	42
Binary Operations on Arrays	43
Modulus Function	44
Summation & General Comments	45

BASIC V For the Acorn Archimedes

8 : Using Colour	**46**
Sixteen-Colour Modes	46
Changing Colours	47
Pointer, Border and Flashing Colours	51
Using the 256-colour modes	52
Using 64 Colours	52
Understanding 256-Colour Modes	54
Redefining the Palette	54
Final Comments	57
9 : Graphics	**61**
New Graphics Commands	61
Fill Routines	65
Relative Co-ordinates	66
Plotting Sprites	66
10 : Archimedes Mouse	**68**
Input from the mouse	69
Further mouse controls	71
Colouring the Mouse Pointer	72
Example Mouse Program	73
11 : Sound	**76**
BASIC Sound Instructions	76
Setting the Stereo Position	77
Setting and Reading the Beat	78
Setting and Reading the Tempo	78
Sound Statement	79
Star Commands	80
12 : Commands	**82**
13 : ARM Assembler	**83**
Calling Machine Code Routines	86
Using CALL with Parameter Passing	88
14 : Operating System Calls	**91**
SYS Calls	91
15 : Miscellaneous Changes	**95**
LINE INPUT	95
ON and OFF	95
QUIT	95

END	96
Mode Changes in Functions	96
Improved PRINT Accuracy	96
Increased Line Number Range	96
Improved COUNT	96

BASIC V For the Acorn Archimedes

BASIC V For the Acorn Archimedes

1 : Introduction

Since the advent of the BBC micro in the autumn of 1981, it has been my view that BBC BASIC is one of the best implementations of this language produced for any computer. There are various reasons for making such a claim, the control of graphics, the access provided to the Operating System, the opportunities for sound, and more. Above all, it is its support for structured programming that most appeals.

Look at almost any program written in BBC BASIC and you will see ample evidence of this approach. Typically, you will find a comparatively short main program, followed by large numbers of functions and procedures, and nary a GOTO or GOSUB in sight. Given that many users of BBC BASIC would not call themselves professional programmers, I take this wide scale adoption of structured programming to provide ample support for its benefits. Prominent among these must be that such programs are eminently more readable and understandable than those which make frequent use of GOTO and GOSUB. Understandable programs are far more likely to work, and much easier to modify in the future, if and when the need arises.

Despite that, there have been a number of omissions even in BBC BASIC until now. For example, the IF...THEN...ELSE statement has often been the source of confusion when used in a nested form. The impossibility of executing any built in loop structure (FOR...NEXT and REPEAT...UNTIL) less than once will also, I am sure, strike a chord in many. These are not the only areas where BBC BASIC is less than perfect.

Despite its shortcomings, BBC BASIC's widespread acceptance, particularly among educational users, has seen the release of BBC BASIC on other machines, notably the RM Nimbus, the Atari ST and the Apple Macintosh. Unfortunately, not all of the features of BBC BASIC that make the language so good, transfer sufficiently well onto other machines.

Now we have the RISC-based Archimedes, Acorn's latest range of personal computers. To accompany the Archimedes, Acorn has released a new version of the BASIC language called BBC BASIC V. BASIC V is clearly an evolutionary step in the development of BBC BASIC. Virtually all that existed before remains, even if some features are implemented quite differently, for example, the software simulation of Teletext mode 7. Many existing BBC BASIC programs will run without modification on an Archimedes, using ARM BASIC, not just under the 6502 emulator. In many cases they benefit from the enormous increase in speed that the Archimedes range provides.

BASIC V For the Acorn Archimedes

The thing that really sets BASIC V apart from previous versions is the addition of several important programming structures, WHILE...ENDWHILE, CASE...ENDCASE for example, and, not before its time, a fully block-structured IF...THEN...ELSE. There is also a full range of matrix operations, improved parameter passing to functions and procedures, support for the new 256 colour modes, and the Archimedes palette of 4096 colours. This list by no means exhausts the new additions - a wealth of smaller details has substantially improved an already respected language.

Despite all these new features, there is, I believe, a very real danger that many Archimedes users, accustomed to using BBC BASIC on the BBC micro and other machines, will fail to appreciate the much richer programming environment that now exists with BASIC V. Thus this book, which might seem to have an obvious theme in documenting and explaining all that is new about BASIC V, will we hope also serve to show just what riches await the adventurous and imaginative programmer.

Another point to consider here is the openness of the Archimedes, and indeed any BBC micro. There is no difficulty, as with some machines, in accessing from BASIC the many Operating System routines, both within the OS ROM and in the many relocatable modules used to extend the Operating System. There was a great temptation to stray from the straight and narrow and attempt to cover all of these areas as well.

What I have done is to explain, as fully as possible, all the new features, large and small, of BASIC V itself. In addition, I have covered the means which BASIC provides to the programmer to go outside the confines of the BASIC language in order to exploit the whole of the Archimedes system. Apart from a few enticing tasters, these wider aspects are beyond the scope of this book. The boundary that I have drawn may at times see arbitrary, but fundamentally I believe that it has a sound logical basis.

I have included plenty of short examples, and tried to ensure that the new features of BASIC V are frequently included in them. Much can be learnt from other people's programs. Inevitably, you will find some new ideas being used before they have been fully described, and you may wish to follow any such new ideas where you come across them. This should cause no problems. The chapters do form a logical order, but each one is largely self-contained.

The book is aimed at those who have reasonable familiarity with programming in BBC BASIC. This is not a book for complete beginners, nor is it necessarily addressed to those who find their greatest interest deep in the bits and bytes of assembler. It is for the very large majority of Archimedes users who simply want to exploit this super machine to the best of their ability.

2 : Operators

Our investigation of BASIC V starts with a comparatively low-key subject, but one which forms the core of so many instructions. All programming languages use a variety of operators. Obvious examples are the arithmetic operators such as multiply (*) and divide (/). There are also logical operators such as AND and OR, and there are relational operators such as 'greater than' (>) and 'not equal to' (<>).

Some symbols can have more than one meaning, determined by the context in which they are used. For example, the equals symbol (=) is used both as a relational operator (eg, IF x=y THEN ...) and as an assignment operator (eg, disc=b^2-4*a*c). Similarly the plus sign (+) is used both for the addition of numbers and the concatenation (joining together) or strings (A=B+C and A$=B$+C$).

New Assignment Operators

BASIC V introduces a number of additional operators. There are two new assignment operators for incrementing or decrementing the values of variables. Examples are:

```
X+=1:Y+=1 : Increment X and Y by one.
X-=FNmouse : Decrement X by the value returned by FNmouse.
```

The variable on the left of the 'plus/equals' (or 'minus/equals') sign is incremented (or decremented) by the value of the expression to the right of this sign. The examples above are equivalent to:

```
X=X+1:Y=Y+1
X=X-FNmouse
```

There is one small but important difference between the two forms, the old and the new. On the Archimedes, a statement like:

```
X=X+1
```

is sufficient to *declare* the variable X with an initial value of zero, which is then incremented. The new form:

```
X+=1
```

does not initialise X, and unless this has been explicitly undertaken beforehand, an error will result ("Mistake").

9

BASIC V For the Acorn Archimedes

New Unary Operators

Unary operators are those that operate on a single value rather than two, as do most operators. Minus (-) is a unary operator because we can write statements like:

```
X1=-X
```

where the minus sign is applied to the value of x, and the resulting value is assigned to the variable X1. The minus sign, confusingly, can also be used as a binary operator, (binary meaning that it has t o operands), when used to indicate the operation of subtraction. Other examples of unary operators that already exist are the tilde (~) and ampersand (&) for conversion to and from hexadecimal formats, and the so-called indirection operators (?, ! and $), the first two of which can be used both as unary or binary operators.

BASIC V adds two new unary operators to those already available. These are 'per cent' (%) to indicate a binary value (just as & indicates hexadecimal) and 'bar' (|) to specify 5-byte floating-point indirection. Thus %101101 is the same as 45 (decimal) and &2D (hex). You will also find that ~%101101 will convert the binary format directly into a hexadecimal format (&2D). The main purpose of this operator is to allow constants to be specified in binary where this is more appropriate. For example, if you want to convert a character (entered as either upper or lower case) into upper case only, the following conversion will suffice:

```
char%=GET AND %11011111
```

Since the AND is specifically required to operate in a bit-wise manner, specifying the second operand in binary makes much more sense. Unfortunately, there is no binary equivalent of the tilde (~) for conversion of numbers into a binary format for display and printing.

The other new unary operator extends the indirection operators to include floating point explicitly. Thus, given a suitable memory location (say P%), the following assignments may be made:

```
?P%=123 byte - maximum value 255
!P%=32666 integer - standard four-byte format
|P%=3.1415927 floating point - standard five-byte
$P%="Hello" string - terminated by a zero
```

Unlike the byte and integer indirection operators, the new floating-point indirection operator may only be used as a unary operator. Thus:

```
P%!5=3.1415927
```

is illegal and will generate the error message "Mistake". However, there is no constraint on using the new operator in the form:

```
!(P%+5)=3.1415927
```

This form, therefore, provides an even better alternative to the '!' operator for copying sections of memory from one location to another, by moving five rather than four bytes at a time.

New Binary Operators

As already explained, binary operators are those which require two operands, and are nothing in particular to do with the binary number system. BASIC V now provides three shift operators as follows:

```
X >> b   Arithmetic shift right
X >>> b  Logical shift right
X << b   Logical shift left
```

The first operand is the value to be shifted, and the second specifies the number of bits. The User Guide gives scant information on the precise action performed by these operators and yet the detail of how they work is crucial. In principle, shifting 1 bit to the right is equivalent to dividing the number by 2, while shifting 1 bit to the left is equivalent to multiplying by the same amount.

When applying a shift, BASIC converts any number into a 32-bit format. These operations can be applied to floating point numbers and variables provided that their values do not go beyond the accepted integer range (-2147483648 to 214783647 decimal, &FFFFFFFF to &7FFFFFFF hex). For this reason it is best to confine these operations to integer variables and their values only. In any case, it makes little sense to apply what are essentially bit-wise operations to floating point numbers held in mantissa/exponent format (often called 'scientific' notation).

The arithmetic shift right preserves the sign, while the number, positive or negative, becomes smaller and smaller. This is illustrated in figure 2.1. If the operation is repeated indefinitely, then a steady state is ultimately reached with the smallest positive (0) or negative (-1) number that can be represented. Because BASIC uses a twos complement notation, -1 (decimal) is represented by an all ones value in binary (&FFFFFFFF in hex). Further arithmetic shifts to the right merely serve to preserve the existing number.

11011001	10110110	00111000	10011001
after >>4 becomes:			
11111101	10011011	01100011	10001001

Figure 2.1. An example of an arithmetic shift right

BASIC V For the Acorn Archimedes

Contrast this with what happens when a logical shift right is applied. This time the 32 bits are treated as an unsigned value and all bits are shifted to the right, with zero being introduced from the left. Repeated applications of the logical shift right will therefore always result ultimately in a zero value, regardless of the starting value or what it represents.

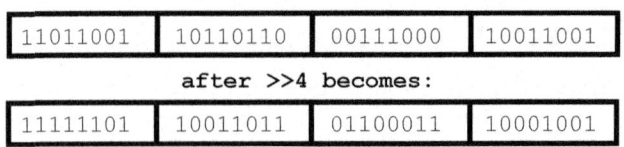

Figure 2.2. An example of a logical shift right

There is only one shift left and this does not preserve the sign (if any), while zeros are shifted in from the right. Since a '1' in the left-most bit position indicates a negative number in twos complement notation, you are likely to find that any number apparently oscillates between positive and negative if a shift left is applied repeatedly.

The shortest way to try this out for yourself is to use the following in immediate mode and look at the results:

```
X%=45:REPEAT:P.~X%,X%:X%=X%>>1:UNTIL FALSE
```

This will produce a list of both hexadecimal and decimal values as the value initially assigned to X% is progressively shifted one bit at a time. Just substitute whatever integer value you want to try in place of the 45 (and you will need to substitute both negative and positive values to see properly what is happening), and replace the '>>' by either of the other two shift operators ('>>>' and '<<') as you wish. Use ESCAPE to terminate execution.

A more sophisticated version of this routine, which prompts for the initial number and shift operator, is listed at the end of this chapter. The output is displayed in hexadecimal and decimal formats in order to provide the maximum information. Try both positive and negative numbers with all three types of shift operator in turn.

As a simple example of the application of shift operators in BASIC V, consider the selection of colours in the 256-colour modes. If the variables red%, green% and blue% each specify the amount of these primary colours (in the range of 0 to 3), then any one of 64 colours may be selected by writing:

```
COLOUR blue%<<4 + green%<<2 + red%
```

The 64 colours may be expanded to 256 by the addition of tint, in which case the statement above has TINT tint%<<4 added to the end.

Swapping Variables

Although not strictly an operator, we complete this chapter by looking at the new SWAP command. This allows the values of two variables (including elements or arrays), or two complete arrays, to be swapped. The typical statement found in sort routines:

```
IF data(I%)>data(I%+1) THEN PROCswap(I%)
```

where PROCswap is defined as:

```
DEF PROCswap(i%)
LOCAL temp
temp=data(i%):data(i%)=data(i%+1):data(i%+1)=temp
ENDPROC
```

can now be written very simply as:

```
IF data(I%)>data(I%+1) THEN SWAP data(I%),data(I%+1)
```

Other examples of the SWAP statement could include:

```
SWAP name1$,name2$
SWAP newx,oldx
SWAP matrix1(),matrix2()
```

Values being swapped must both be of the same type (integer, floating point, or string). In the case of complete arrays, the number of subscripts and the upper limits of the two arrays are also swapped. Thus, if two arrays are dimensioned as:

```
DIM fred(20), freda(30,30)
```

then, after executing SWAP fred(),freda(), it would be as though the two arrays had been dimensioned as:

```
DIM fred(30,30), freda(20)
```

Listing 2.1. Demonstration of Shift Operations.

```
 10 REM >Chap2-1
100 MODE 7:VDU14
110 PRINTTAB(12,1)"SHIFT OPERATORS"
120 VDU28,0,24,39,3
130 ON ERROR PROCerror:IF err% THEN END
140 DIM shift$(3):shift$(1)=">>"
150 shift$(2)=">>>":shift$(3)="<<"
160 REPEAT:CLS
170 INPUT''"Enter any integer value: " X%
180 PRINT'TAB(5)"1. Arithmetic shift right"
190 PRINT'TAB(5)"2. Logical shift right"
```

BASIC V For the Acorn Archimedes

```
200 PRINT'TAB(5)"3. Shift left
210 INPUT'"Enter operation required (1, 2, 3): " P%
220 PRINT'TAB(5)"Hex"TAB(23)"Decimal"'
230 REPEAT
240 PRINT ~X%,SPC7,X%
250 X%=EVAL(STR$(X%)+shift$(P%)+"1")
260 UNTIL X%=0 OR X%=-1
270 PRINT ~X%,SPC7,X%
280 PRINT "Press any key to continue";:G=GET
290 UNTIL FALSE
300 END
310 :
320 DEF PROCerror:err%=FALSE
330 IF ERR<>20 THEN
340 err%=TRUE
350 PRINT REPORT$;" at line ";ERL
360 ENDIF
370 ENDPROC
```

3 : String Handling

String Functions

Probably the most frequently used string functions in BBC BASIC are LEFT$, MID$ and RIGHT$. In BASIC V all three functions have enhanced functionality offering additional facilities. The existing interpretations remain as before. Both LEFT$ and RIGHT$ may now take a single character string as their sole parameter. For example, given:

```
data$="Appalachians"
```

then the assignment:

```
one$=LEFT$(data$)
```

would assign the character string "Appalachian" to the variable one$. Effectively, the string specified is reduced by one character from the right, and avoids the previous requirement of:

```
one$=LEFT$(data$,LEN(data$)-1)
```

The equivalent use of RIGHT$ is used as follows:

```
two$=RIGHT$(data$)
```

and would result in two$ being assigned the right-most character of data$. Thus given a string data$, there is a simple relationship between these functions in the form:

```
data$=LEFT$(data$)+RIGHT$(data$)
```

One possible use of these new formats is in stripping characters from the right-hand end of a string. This process is the reverse of padding out a string for justification or for file handling using fixed-length fields. For example, a suitable function could be written as:

```
DEF FNstrip(data$,pad$)
WHILE RIGHT$(data$)=pad$
data$=LEFT$(data$)
ENDWHILE
```

where pad$ is the character selected previously for padding out the string in the first place (this could be space - ASCII 32 - or any other character depending on the context). Notice, too, the efficiency of the new WHILE construction for this purpose (see Chapter Four), compared with REPEAT... UNTIL. Even if the string specified contains no pad characters the function still works correctly, where as this would need to be treated as a special case

BASIC V For the Acorn Archimedes

using REPEAT...UNTIL, which always executes a loop at least once.

A new variation on the MID$ function has also been provided. It differs from other forms in that the MID$ function appears on the left-hand side of an assignment statement. Again, this is most easily explained by means of an example. Given:

```
town$="Newcastle-under-Lyme"
```

the assignment:

```
MID$(town$,11,10)="upon-Tyne"
```

would result in the variable town$ containing the string "Newcastle-upon-Tyne".

To the right of the equals sign may be any expression which evaluates to a string. The characters are used to replace specified characters within the string variable supplied as the first parameter in the MID$ function. The second parameter indicates the position of the first character to be replaced, while the third parameter, which is optional, specifies the maximum number of characters to be replaced. If this third parameter is omitted, then all the following characters may potentially be replaced. Note, however, that it is the length of the string contained within the first string variable that determines how many characters will be replaced, not the number of characters to the right of the '=' sign. If the example above had been given the other way round as:

```
town$="Newcastle-upon-Tyne"
```

then the assignment:

```
MID$(town$,11,9)="under-Lyme"
```

would result in town$ containing just "Newcastle-under-Lyme". Starting on the 11th character of the original string assigned to town$, there are only 9 characters marked to be replaced. The string "under-Lyme" contains 10 characters, so the last one remains unused.

Another way of looking at this use of MID$ is to consider how the same function might have been written previously. Thus:

```
MID$(string1$,p,q)=string2$
```

is the equivalent of:

```
string1$=LEFT(string1$,p-1)+MID$(string2$,p,q)+
                RIGHT$(string1$,LEN(string1$)-p-q+1)
```

Although this conveys quite well the idea of taking the left-hand part, replacing the middle part, and then keeping the right-hand part, this would more likely be written as:

```
string1$=LEFT(string1$,p-1)+MID$(string2$,p,q)+
                                  MID$(string1$,p+q)
```

String Handling in Files

Two further string functions have been enhanced in BASIC V for use where reading data from files. The function:

```
GET$#C
```

will read a string of characters from an open file until a linefeed (CHR$10), carriage return (CHR$13), null character (CHR$0) or until end-of-file (EOF# returns true) is found. However, the maximum number of characters that may be read in cannot exceed 255. As with other instructions for reading and writing data, the instruction must specify the channel number of the file to be used, which should already be open, for example:

```
data$=GET$#C
```

The ability to read a string from a file with GET$# has been complemented by a new version of the BPUT# function, which may now also be used to write a string to a file. The format is:

```
BPUT#C,data$
```

where C is the channel number of the file to be used and data$ is any expression which evaluates to a character string. The resultant string plus a terminating linefeed character (ASCII 10) is sent to the file. If the struct specified is terminated by a semi-colon as in:

```
BPUT#C,data$;
```

then the terminating linefeed character is omitted. In either case, the maximum string length is again 255 characters.

Organisation and Allocation of String Storage

The organisation and allocation of memory for string storage in BASIC V has been completely changed compared with the system used for BBC BASIC. This system was potentially wasteful of space if character strings of varying sizes were to be assigned to the same string variable at frequent intervals. If a character string was to be assigned to a string variable, then new space would be allocated from remaining free memory f it was larger than the space previously allocated to that string variable. The old memory allocation would then be 'thrown away', and would effectively be lost to the program for any future use.

Thus, a situation in which progressively larger strings are assigned to a string variable will cause new memory to be assigned each time and the old allocation wasted. This system was 'improved' by two particular techniques. First, new memory was always allocated at four bytes more than the immediate requirement to allow some room for future expansion of that string. Second, if the existing memory was contiguous with free space then it was kept and extended. BASIC programmers, aware of the resulting memory problems, developed various techniques to minimise the effects. The principal method used was to assign to any frequently used string variable, a character string of the maximum length that the program would be called upon to handle.

New Memory Allocation System

BASIC V implements a totally new method of string storage. When a new character string is to be assigned to a string variable which is greater in length than the space already allocated, then that space is de-allocated and new string space used. However, the discarded string space is now added to a linked list of similar space of the same length. The system maintains a set of linked lists, each one containing string space of the same size.

When new string space is required, BASIC first checks with the appropriate linked list and if there is an entry it takes it. If no space of the right size is available it then assigns string space from free memory. The new system will still extend existing string space if this is contiguous with free memory. However, only the current string length (CLEN) is stored, whereas before, both this and maximum string length (MLEN) were stored for every string. This represents a useful memory saving, particularly for string arrays.

The new system is intended to reduce significantly the loss of memory through the inability to re-use discarded string space, while the multiple linked lists of free string space provide a faster method of locating and assigning string space as required.

String space is always allocated in multiples of words (not bytes), and strings are always aligned on word boundaries. The new system improves on the previous system of memory allocation, but is still less than perfect. Most programs are still likely to generate unusable string space, but the much greater memory of the Archimedes (compared with the older BBC Micros) should reduce the likely incidence of insufficient memory. Certainly there is now much less advantage to be gained from the previous technique of initialising a string to the longest length needed.

4 : Control Structures

All programs consist essentially of two types of instruction, those that instruct the computer to perform some sort of action, such as the addition of two numbers or the printing of a text message, and those that control the order of execution of instructions in a program. Although BASIC has generally been weak in such control structures, BBC BASIC has traditionally provided more facilities than most.

Three control structures exist, namely FOR...NEXT, REPEAT...UNTIL and IF...THEN...ELSE. The first two provide alternative methods of controlling loops, but in both cases the body of the loop, that is the group of instructions contained within the loop, is always executed at least once. Even in instances where a FOR...NEXT loop is used logically one would not expect this to happen, but it still does. This results from the fact that, in both structures, the test to determine whether the body of the loop should be executed (again) is only reached after the loop has been executed at least once. The problem can be avoided, but only artificially.

The existing IF...THEN...ELSE statement also suffers in not providing a true block-structured format, and unless used with extreme care it is extraordinarily easy to become lost in the logic of this instruction when nested to any degree.

BASIC V extends the range of control structures considerably. In particular there is now a CASE statement, in effect a multi-branched IF...THEN...ELSE. A new variant of the IF...THEN...ELSE statement itself has been added, which implements proper block structuring, and a new WHILE...ENDWHILE structure provides a loop format, where the test comes at the commencement of the loop rather than at the end.

WHILE Loops

Students of computer science will be quite familiar with the concept of a WHILE loop, which is considered to be one of the most fundamental (and most natural) of control structures. It takes the form:

```
WHILE   <condition>:<statements>
  <statements>
  <statements>
ENDWHILE
```

BASIC V For the Acorn Archimedes

While the specified condition remains true, the statements between WHILE and ENDWHILE will continue to be executed. The statements may be on the same line as the WHILE or on separate lines. For example, you might write:

```
100 Sum=0:k=1
110 WHILE Sum<=10:Sum=Sum+1/k:k=K+1:ENDWHILE
120 PRINT k
130 END
```

This program determines the number of terms in the series:

```
1+1/2+1/3+1/4+1/5+....
```

required to produce a sum greater than 10. The great advantage of the WHILE loop is that if the condition fails (ie, returns a value FALSE) the very first time it is tested, then the following statements will not be executed at all, just what we would logically expect.

Here is another very simple example:

```
i=1
WHILE (i<max AND list(i)<>key):i+=1:ENDWHILE
```

The coding assumes that an array called list() has been dimensioned to size 'max', and searches the list for an element whose value matches that of 'key'. When the loop terminates, 'i' contains the value of the matched element, or is set to the value of 'max' if no match has been found. Notice how, in this example, more work is done in evaluating the condition than in the body of the loop. This is not uncommon.

WHILE...ENDWHILE structures may also be nested in the same way as FOR loops and REPEAT...UNTIL loops. Each loop must be correctly terminated with an ENDWHILE statement. Likewise, the statements within a WHILE... ENDWHILE construction may include other forms of control structure such as CASE...ENDCASE, REPEAT...UNTIL and FOR...NEXT.

Block-Structured IF

BBC BASIC has always supported and IF...THEN...ELSE statement, but this has been limited in two separate but linked ways, which particularly affect the nested use of IF...THEN...ELSE. The complete structured must be contained within a single line of BASIC (thus limited to a maximum of 255 characters), while the logical interpretation of nested IF...THEN...ELSE statements frequently leads to confusion. As a result, many instances of more complex usage often fail to work correctly, and much time can be wasted in sorting this out.

For example, consider the following:

```
IF (B^2-4*a*c)<>0 THEN IF (b^-4*a*c)>0 THEN PRINT"Roots are
real" ELSE IF (B^2-4*a*c)<0 THEN PRINT "Roots are complex" ELSE
PRINT "Roots are equal"
```

Now most programmers are familiar with solving quadratic equations, and can therefore follow what the above code is intended to achieve, but could you say with confidence whether this form of coding is correct? The new block-structured form of IF...THEN...ELSE should help to bring new clarity to such situations as we shall see. It also removes the 255 character limitation on the length of such statements by allowing them to spread over as many separate lines of BASIC as required. In addition, the old form of IF...THEN...ELSE is still retained, and may continue to be used wherever appropriate. Indeed, its simpler form should always be used if possible.

The syntax of the block-structured IF takes the following form:

```
IF <condition> THEN
  <statements>
ELSE
  <statements>
END IF
```

The structure is reasonably flexible, but the following constraints must always be observed. The THEN must be the last item on a line, while ELSE and ENDIF must be the first items on their respective lines. In addition, the ELSE clause is optional, the ENDIF is not. Thus, the example on the solution of quadratic equations could now be coded as:

```
IF (b^2-a*c)<>0 THEN
  IF (b^2-4*a*c)>0 THEN
    PRINT "Roots are real"
  ENDIF
  ELSE
  IF (b^2-4*a*c)<0 THEN
    PRINT "Roots are complex"
  ENDIF
  ELSE
    PRINT "Roots are equal"
ENDIF
```

Each line given above would be written as a separate numbered line of BASIC. There are two nested IF...THEN...ELSE constructions, the outer one concerned with whether the formula equates to zero or not, and, in the case of a non-zero value, a further IF...THEN...ELSE to distinguish between positive and negative values. You will probably find that it still helps to indent some of the lines as above to make the logic quite clear.

The example I have used above, and in particular the manner in which I have expressed it, is somewhat artificial, though it serves to illustrate the point.

Keeping the same overall structure, the block-structured version could be more succinctly written as:

```
IF (b^2-4*a*c)<>0 THEN
  IF (b^2-4*a*c)>0 THEN PRINT"Roots are real"
  IF (b^2-4*a*c)<0 THEN PRINT"Roots are complex"
ELSE
  PRINT"Roots are equal"
ENDIF
```

There are, no doubt, many other variations and it is perfectly possible to code the example using the simple IF...THEN...ELSE construction, all on one line of BASIC:

```
IF (B^2-4*a*c)=0 THEN PRINT"Roots are equal"
  ELSE IF (B^2-4*a*c)>0 THEN PRINT"Roots are real"
  ELSE IF (B^2-4*a*c)<0 THEN PRINT"Roots are complex"
```

If you are using the simple form of IF...THEN...ELSE, you will generally find that else followed by IF (as in the example above) gives no cause for concern, but that THEN followed by IF (as in the original coding) frequently leads to confusion and incorrect logic.

The moral is to think carefully about the logic of the algorithm you are about to code. There is every reason to retain the simpler form of IF...THEN...ELSE where this is clear and unambiguous. If you need to exceed the limited capacity of one line of BASIC, or the logic is more than the simpler form can adequately cope with, bring the block-standard form into play.

The CASE Statement

A CASE statement is, in effect, a generalised form of IF...THEN...ELSE. The latter essentially allows a program to distinguish between two alternatives based on whether a condition is true or false. The CASE statement allows the condition (or state) which is to be tested to have as many alternative values as you wish, and specifies the action to be followed in each 'case'.

The syntax for the CASE statement takes the following form:

```
CASE <expression> OF
  WHEN <states>: <statements>
  WHEN <states>: <statements>
   . . . . . . . . . . . . . .
   . . . . . . . . . . . . . .
  OTHERWISE <statements>
ENDCASE
```

A simple example will help to make this clear. The Archimedes mouse, for example, has three buttons generally referred to as select, menu and adjust. Thus a routine to provide mouse control in a program could be written as:

```
MOUSE x,y,z
CASE z OF
  WHEN 4: PROCselect
  WHEN 2: PROCmenu
  WHEN 1: PROCadjust
ENDCASE
```

This coding would probably be embedded in some sort of loop so that the program can continually follow the movement of the mouse. The value of z determines which mouse button has been pressed by the user (BASIC allocated 4 for select, 2 for menu and 1 for adjust). The three WHEN statements each call an appropriate procedure corresponding to the button pressed.

BASIC goes through the list of WHEN statements until it finds a match between the value specified and the value of the expression following CASE. The instructions specified by tat WHEN statement are then executed and control passes to the first statement following the ENDCASE, even if more matches exist in subsequent WHEN statements, as yet untested. This is important to understand. You could not use this example, as it stands, to test for two buttons being pressed together. Hence, however many WHEN statements are specified in a CASE construction, only one, if any, will be executed. Of course, a CASE statement may produce no match at all.

The WHEN statement can specify more than one value, and these are separated by commas. With the mouse, pressing two or more buttons together produces values which are the sum of the values that would have resulted from pressing the same buttons individually. Adding the following line could cater for any two or three buttons being pressed by mistake:

```
WHEN 3,5,6,7: PROCerror(z)
```

In such as case, BASIC seeks for a match between the value of the CASE expression and any of the values listed after WHEN. These alternatives are simply separated by commas.

It is also possible to include an OTHERWISE clause in a CASE statement. This must follow the last WHEN statement in a list and stipulates the action to be taken if no specific match occurs. For example, we could package up our whole mouse routine as follows:

```
REPEAT
MOUSE x,y,z
CASE z OF
  WHEN 4: PROCselect
```

BASIC V For the Acorn Archimedes

```
   WHEN 2:  PROCmenu
   WHEN 1:  PROCadjust
   WHEN 7:  exit%=TRUE
   OTHERWISE PROCerror(z)
 ENDCASE
UNTIL exit%
```

There is now a loop which repeatedly returns information about the position of the mouse pointer and the state of the mouse buttons. Appropriate action is determined by a CASE statement in response to the buttons pressed.

When using the CASE statement, CASE...OF must be the last item on a line of BASIC, while WHEN, OTHERWISE and ENDCASE must be the first objects on a line. Note also that a colon is essential to terminate the list of possible matches in a WHEN statement, though no colon is required after OTHERWISE (as there is no list here).

It is worthwhile to consider the workings of the CASE statements further, as there are alternative ways of using such statements which may not be immediately obvious. The CASE statement is concerned with finding a match between the values of expressions, where the term expression also includes constants. Thus an equation is an expression, so is z and so is 5.2 (with this interpretation). One of the expressions to be matched, the key expression if you like, is specified after CASE, and other lists of expressions are given after each WHEN. In the examples so far, the key expression has been given a simple variable, and the WHEN expressions as constants.

Furthermore, expressions may produce a numeric value, a string value or a logical value. For example, a typical command-driven system for a file handling program might have the following structure:

```
REPEAT:exit%=FALSE
command$=FNmenu
CASE command$ OF
  WHEN "OPEN":      PROCopen_file
  WHEN "CLOSE":     PROCclose_file
  WHEN "ADD":       PROCadd_record
  WHEN "DELETE":    PROCdelete_record
  WHEN "UPDATE":    PROCupdate_record
  WHEN "DISPLAY":   PROCdisplay_record
  WHEN "EXIT":      exit%=TRUE
  OTHERWISE         PROCerror
ENDCASE
UNTIL exit%
```

It is natural to think of the WHEN statements as specifying instances of the CASE...OF expression, but it is quite possible to turn it round, so that this becomes a (single) instance of a WHEN expression. Consider the following routine:

```
MOUSE x,y,z
CASE TRUE OF
  WHEN FNin(x,y,z,120,100,200,100): PROCload
  WHEN FNin(x,y,z,400,100,200,100): PROCsave
  WHEN FNin(x,y,z,680,100,200,100): PROCedit
  WHEN FNin(x,y,z,960,100,200,100): PROCexit
ENDCASE
```

Assume that the screen display consists of four boxes across the foot of the screen labelled LOAD, SAVE, EDIT and EXIT. FNin is a function with seven parameters. The first three are the position of the mouse pointer and status of the mouse buttons. The other four are the x and y co-ordinates of the bottom left-hand corner and the width and height of a rectangular area on the screen. FNin returns a logical value of TRUE if the mouse pointer is within the specified area with the select button depressed. The CASE statement given above is one way of detecting which part of the screen is being pointed to before taking appropriate action.

The CASE construction is an important addition to BASIC V, one that will do much to avoid some of the more tortuous programming previously required to meet the need for a multiple-choice structure. It will also do much to enhance further the reputation of BBC BASIC. It does require the programmer to exercise careful consideration of its use, both in getting the syntax correct and in applying its logic in the most effective way. With practice you should find that CASE...OF becomes a frequently used feature in your programs.

5 : Procedures & Functions

In contrast to many implementations of BASIC, the BBC version of this language has always provided good procedure and function handling, including multi-line definitions and, most importantly, parameter passing. Indeed, programs written in BBC BASIC are normally characterised by their frequent use of both of these structures, leading to highly logical and readable programs. That BBC BASIC encourages such a structured approach to programming is to be commended, and in this respect at least puts this version of BASIC on a part with such languages as C and Pascal.

However, as with some of the other better features of BBC BASIC, the use of procedures and functions has still been limited in certain respects. In particular, parameters could only be used to pass values to a procedure or function, and not for the return of values to the calling program (although a function can, separately, return a single value). Secondly, there has been no provision at all for passing arrays as parameters. Both of these restrictions have disappeared in BASIC V, and a number of other enhancements, particularly with regard to the use of libraries, further improve the power and flexibility of functions and procedures in BBC BASIC. There have also been substantial improvements affecting error handling within procedures and functions, but these are dealt with separately in the next chapter.

Passing Parameters

Let us consider a very simple example of a procedure or function and see how this benefits from the enhancements to parameter passing in BASIC V. Suppose we want to order the values contained in two variables. Previously, the only way of encoding this would have been to write a function to determine if the two values should be swapped, and then to re-assign the values if necessary. For this assume the two numbers to be re-ordered are contained in variables A and B, and that we wish the larger to be in A and the smaller in B:

```
IF FNswap(A,B) THEN temp=A:A=B:B=temp
:
DEF FNswap(A,B)
IF B>A THEN =TRUE ELSE =FALSE
```

It is impossible to keep to a strict use of parameters and LOCAL variables, and perform the swap entirely within the procedure or function definition, because of the inability to return more than a single value, and that only with

BASIC V For the Acorn Archimedes

a function. As a result, the coding above is restricted to ordering the contents of the two variables A and B only. In fact, because of these limitations, the above example might as well be written as:

```
IF B>A THEN temp=A:A=B:B=temp
```

but this is quite specific to the variables A and B. In BASIC V we could rewrite this all as a procedure as follows:

```
PROCswap(fred1,fred2)
:
DEF PROCswap(RETURN A,RETURN B)
IF B>A THEN SWAP A,B
ENDPROC
```

The procedure definition is entirely self-contained and may be used to swap the contents of any two variables, as with fred1 and fred2 in the example call. Note the use of the new SWAP instruction to simplify matters.

The difference is achieved by the use of the keyword RETURN when defining the procedure. Without this, the only option previously, BASIC treats any formal parameters given in the definition of a procedure or function as being strictly LOCAL to that definition. Thus, when such a function or procedure is called, memory is allocated to those variables and the corresponding values, supplied as part of the call, are assigned to them. This explains why it is possible to make assignments to variables defined as formal parameters in a procedure or function definition. Within such a definition, the formal parameters are treated like any other variables such as LOCAL. On exit from the procedure or function, all such variables, and their values, are lost.

When the keyword RETURN is used in specifying a formal parameter, no local allocation of storage takes place, apart from variables explicitly declared as LOCAL, when the routine is called. Instead, the procedure, or function, is passed a reference to the location of the corresponding data item. Any reference within the procedure definition is directed to the original data item as set up by the calling program. Any assignment to such a formal parameter will, therefore, replace the original data with the new value.

There are two points to note when calling a procedure or function which uses RETURN to define parameters in this way. You cannot then specify actual values as parameters in the procedure or function call - only variables will do. This follows logically from the way in which RETURN parameters are treated. Without a variable there is no reference to pass to the procedure or function.

The second point is that variables passes as RETURN parameters must have been implicitly declared, by assigning them some value, before including them in a procedure call. For example, we might wish a procedure to return the largest and smallest values found in an array (see later for more relevant

BASIC V For the Acorn Archimedes

information on arrays). Such a procedure might be defined as:

```
DEF PROCmaxmin(data(),RETURN max,RETURN min)
LOCAL i,n:n=DIM(data(),1)
max=data(1):min=max
FOR i=2 to n
IF data(i)>max THEN max=data(i)
IF data(i)
```

Note the use of DIM to determine the size of the array passed to the procedure. This technique is described more fully in Chapter Seven. If such a procedure were to be called with a line such as:

```
PROCmaxmin(height(),high,low)
```

in order to find the highest and lowest of a set of heights, then it would need to be preceded by a line similar to:

```
high=0:low=0
```

in order to make the two variables high and low 'known' to BASIC. The values assigned to these variables are quite immaterial, as they are reinitialised within the procedure definition. The purpose is merely to force BASIC to include them in its list of known variables prior to make the procedure call. Arrays (see below) must likewise be dimensioned before being used as parameters to procedures and functions. If these steps are omitted then an error message ("No such variable") will result.

Programmers using BBC BASIC V now have two choices as far as parameter passing to functions and procedures is concerned, call by value (the old method) and call by reference (the new method). Both ave their place in the programmer's repertoire. A clear understanding of the workings and differences between the two methods is, however, essential to avoid subsequent problems in their use.

Passing Arrays as Parameters

In BASIC V, not only has parameter passing to procedures and functions been greatly improved as already explained, but arrays may now also be specified as parameters. As in other instances where complete arrays are referred to in BASIC, an array is specified by its name followed by empty parentheses, thus:

```
PROCsort(data())
```

Not only that, but by using the new applications of the DIM statement (see chapter seven), a procedure or function can itself determine the number of dimensions and the size of each dimension of an array passed to it as a parameter.

28

As an example, consider a simple procedure to sort the elements of an array (assumed one-dimensional) into ascending order. This could be coded as follows:

```
DEF PROCsort(data())
LOCAL i,j,n:n=DIM(data(),1)
FOR i=n-1 TO 1 STEP -1
FOR j=1 TO i
PROC swap(data(j+1),data(j))
NEXT j:NEXT i
ENDPROC
```

This procedure uses just a simple bubble sort, which could certainly be improved upon, but it does illustrate the BASIC elements involved. All variables used within the procedure have been declared as local so that procedure is quite independent. The procedure starts by assigning the size of the array to be sorted to the variable n using the DIM statement to obtain this information. The nested FOR...NEXT loops then perform the sort, using the procedure PROCswap described previously, to compare together consecutive elements in the array.

Following our earlier discussion on calling by reference, you might have expected to see the keyword RETURN included in the procedure definition to so define the array parameter. In fact, arrays in BASIC V may only be called in this way, and RETURN is not needed, though it does not generated an error if included. Acorn says that to call arrays by value could involve large amounts of memory being allocated for local storage requirements, and that a significant amount of time might be needed for copying the contents of the array specified into the local array specified by the formal array procedure.

If you do need to write a procedure or function with an array parameter such that the contents of any array passed will not be altered, you will need to make a separate copy before calling the necessary routine and use the unaltered version on exit. Thus, for example:

```
temp()=A()
PROCsort(temp())
```

After executing these two lines, the array A would remain unchanged, while the array temp contains the same data but in ascending order.

Local Arrays

In addition to the facility for passing arrays as parameters, they may now also be declared local to a procedure or function, as with other variables. The array must first be declared as local and then dimensioned. There is, however,

BASIC V For the Acorn Archimedes

nothing to stop the array being dimensioned dynamically when the procedure or function is called, maybe using a value passed as a parameter, or by determining the size of another array also passed as a parameter (see Chapter Seven). For example:

```
LOCAL localarray()
DIM localarray(DIM(A(),1),DIM(A(),2))
```

would declare 'localarray' as a two dimensional local array with the same dimensions as an array A, presumed passed as a parameter. The use of local arrays also provides an alternative solution to the problem of passing an array, as a parameter, to a procedure or function in such a way that the contents of the array passed remain unchanged. The procedure definition could dimension a local array and then copy the contents of the array passed, as a parameter, into this local copy. For example, a procedure definition might begin:

```
DEF PROCcalculate(data())
LOCAL temp()
DIM temp(DIM(data(),1))
temp()=data()
.  .  .  .  .  .  .
```

The procedure would then continue to process the local copy, leaving the original array unaffected. Remember though, that on exit from the procedure, the entire contents of the local copy will be lost, so this is not a suitable solution in all situations.

Since arrays can rapidly eat up memory, it is always sensible to dimension them dynamically where feasible, and to keep the use of arrays, particularly local arrays, to a minimum. Just consider the amount of memory that would be used by a recursively defined procedure repeatedly declaring a two dimensional real array, even one just 10 x 10.

Procedure and Function Libraries

The other main area where handling of procedures and functions has been improved in BASIC V, is in the introduction of a library facility. Once any specified procedure or function library (and both procedures and functions may be included in any library file), has been loaded, any function or procedure calls which cannot be satisfied from within the main program are checked for within the currently loaded library or libraries.

Using libraries has a number of advantages. There are no worries about line number clashes when library procedures and functions are used. Also, keeping a set of routines as a single file, which can be loaded just by

BASIC V For the Acorn Archimedes

referencing its name, saves all the bother of individually loading and merging previously written routines into a new program.

Of course, this convenience has to be paid for in the memory space used up by each loaded library. Because you will seldom use all the procedures or functions in any one library, more memory will be used than if you had individually selected and included just those routines which the program needs.

A BASIC library is simply a saved BASIC program containing only procedure and function definitions, though REM statements may also be included for documentation. Because of the potential for wasting memory space, you are recommended to keep your library files relatively small. It is also essential that you document your library files to make clear what procedures and functions they contain, what their names are and what parameters they require. It is also highly desirable to make such routines as self-contained as possible, by full use of parameter passing and the use of local variables, to avoid any future conflicts or unexpected side-effects.

There are two separate commands which may be used to load a library, and the precise action taken by each is different. The two commands are INSTALL and LIBRARY, and in each case the command is followed by the name of a library, enclosed in double quotes, or a string variable to which a library name has previously been assigned. For example:

```
INSTALL "Utilities2"
LIBRARY library$
```

The INSTALL command will load any specified library at the top of memory, and move BASIC's stack and the value of HIMEM down. Because of this, INSTALL cannot be used when there is anything on the stack (ie, from within a procedure or function, or inside any kind of loop). In addition, installed libraries may only be removed by quitting BASIC. Libraries loaded with the INSTALL command are relatively permanent in nature, and are est loaded at the very start of a program, or, even better, with a finished application, by including the INSTALL command in an appropriate boot file.

The LIBRARY command, on the other hand, loads a specified library immediately above the program itself, effectively using part of the program's variable storage area. As such, libraries loaded in this way are deleted by any of the commands which clear this area (CLEAR, NEW, RUN, etc). However, the LIBRARY command can be used more dynamically than INSTALL, including its use within procedures and functions which are themselves contained in a library.

A base library may contain a small number of procedures, each of which, when called, loads a further applications-orientated library of additional

BASIC V For the Acorn Archimedes

functions and procedures. This makes for more economical use of memory, but all libraries to be loaded, whether using INSTALL or LIBRARY, must be accessible via the current filing system. For large applications, a hard disc would be most useful.

There are some minor constraints on the use of procedure and function libraries. In particular, they should avoid any line number references as in GOTO or RESTORE. Any such references which are included, will be taken as referring to lines in the 'main' program, with potentially disastrous consequences. References to variables not defined as parameters or local to the procedure should also be avoided.

As a practical aid, the LVAR command will not also show what libraries have been loaded into memory. It does this by listing the first line of each library, and it is therefore highly desirable to make this a REM line containing the library name and any other relevant information. This will then serve to document the library file.

Dynamic Loading of Procedure and Function Libraries

BASIC V under the RISC OS Operating System has been further extended to allow procedure and function libraries to be loaded dynamically on demand. The way to implement this in any program is to declare a string array near the start of the program, and assign to this the names of the relevant libraries (starting with the first element of the array). The system can then be initialised by using the OVERLAY command to specify the name of the array being used as an overlay index. For example:

```
DIM library$(8)
library$(1)="Mathslib.hyp1"
library$(2)="Mathslib.hyp2"
library$(3)="Mathslib.stats1"
library$(4)="Mathslib.stats2"
OVERLAY library()
```

When BASIC encounters the OVERLAY command, it reserves an area of user RAM large enough for the biggest library stored in the specified index array. From then on, when a procedure or function is called, BASIC will first search the current program, then any LIBRARYs, then any INSTALLed libraries, and finally any OVERLAY libraries starting with the OVERLAY area. If the procedure or function called is in an OVERLAY library, then this will be loaded dynamically into the overlay area at that time. Clearly, all OVERLAY libraries must be accessible when running programs using this command.

6 : Error Handling

In the past, most BASIC programmers have largely ignored the error handling provided by BBC BASIC, with the exception of a few instances such as trapping ESCAPE and some disc errors. The reason for this state of affairs is that any error trapped by BASIC caused the stack to be zeroed, with a total consequent loss of all stored information relating to functions, procedures and loops of any kind. Given the highly structured nature of most programs written in BBC BASIC, the chances that a program will be executing a function or procedure, or be within a loop, when an error occurs, are likely to be quite high.

As an example, BBC BASIC will detect any attempt to divide by zero, and generate a corresponding error. Because of the problems resulting from the use of error trapping, most programmers cater for this possibility themselves by checking for a zero (or very small) divisor before executing a divide operation.

BASIC V now provides additional error handling facilities which avoid all the previous problems. At any point in a program, a local error trap can be established, saving the pointer to the previous error-trapping status on the stack. Should an error occur, the current error-handling routine will be invoked with no loss of stack information. Once a routine, for which there is local error handling, has been executed, the pointer to the previously effective error trapping status can be retrieved from the stack and reinstated as the current error handling routine.

Using these facilities, truly hierarchical error-handling systems can be readily established. Although local error handling may be incorporated at any point within a program, it is clearly ideally suited to error handling within procedures and functions. Given the highly structured nature of most BBC BASIC programs, global error trapping (to handle escape for example) might be established early in a program, with each function and procedure containing its own error handling routine whenever appropriate.

It is important to realise, however, that when any local error handling routine is active, all errors will be passed to that routine, including those which we might ideally wish to be handled by a more global routine. It is only too easy to forget this and assume that a local error handling routine will only handle specific local errors.

Local Error Trapping

BASIC V For the Acorn Archimedes

Let's look at what the new instructions are in BASIC v and then consider how best to use them. The original ON error statement remains as before and, as before, the occurrence of any error corrupts the stack as already described. A new statement, ON ERROR LOCAL, with the same syntax, is now provided, which does not corrupt the stack in the event of an error. Furthermore, local error may now be used to save the existing error trapping status on the stack before establishing a local error-handling routine. restore error, placed at the end of a routine or section of code, will restore the previously saved error status. In practice, restore error is not strictly necessary on exit from a procedure or function, but it will cause no problems if it is included.

Suppose, as an example, we want to write a procedure which will plot the graph of a function specified as a string. A complete program including such a procedure could be written as follows:

Listing 6.1 Plot program with no error trapping.

```
  10 REM >Chap6-1
 100 MODE 12
 110 REPEAT
 120 INPUT F$,X,Y,I
 130 PROCplot(X,Y,I,F$)
 140 G=GET:CLS
 150 UNTIL FALSE
 160 END
 170 :
1000 DEF PROCplot(Ox,Oy,inc,f$)
1010 LOCAL x,y
1020 MOVE 0,Oy:DRAW 1279,Oy
1030 MOVE Ox,1023:DRAW Ox,0
1040 ORIGIN Ox,Oy:a=-Ox/100:b=(1279-Ox)/100
1050 MOVE -2*Ox,0
1060 FOR x=a TO b STEP inc
1070 y=EVAL(f$)
1080 DRAW 100*x,100*y
1090 NEXT x101100 ORIGIN 0,0
1110 ENDPROC
```

The procedure has four parameters, the position of the origin of the graph on the screen (assuming that the origin is initially in its default position at the bottom left-hand corner), the increment in x to be used when plotting, and the function (of x) itself. The procedure draws in the x and y axis, moves the origin to its new position and then plots the graph using a FOR...next loop. The local variables a and b are the calculated start and end points on the x axis relative to the new origin. Before plotting of the graph begins, a move is made beyond the left-hand edge of the screen ready to commence plotting the

BASIC V For the Acorn Archimedes

graph, using draw. On exit from the procedure, the origin is returned to its default position. Incidentally, note the use of the new statement origin, dealt with more fully in Chapter Nine.

There are many alternative ways in which this procedure could have been written, but this version will suffice for our needs. If we call the procedure, having first cleared the screen in a suitable mode, with the following procedure call:

```
PROCplot(625,512,0.125,3*SIN(x)+SIN(3*x))
```

then the graph will be correctly, and quickly, drawn. Note the lower case 'x' to fit in with the procedure definition. If, however, we try this function:

```
PROCplot(625,512,0.25,10*(SIN(x)/x))
```

then the error message "Division by zero..." will result when the graph reaches the origin. The procedure can trap this situation by using local error trapping. What then happens is up to the programmer - we'll assume we just skip over the contentious value and go on to the next one. The revised procedure appears as listing 6.2.

Listing 6.2 Revised plot procedure with local error trapping.

```
1000 DEF PROCplot(Ox,Oy,inc,f$)
1010 LOCAL x,y
1020 LOCAL ERROR
1030 MOVE 0,Oy:DRAW 1279,Oy
1040 MOVE Ox,1023:DRAW Ox,0
1050 ORIGIN Ox,Oy:a=-Ox/100:b=(1279-Ox)/100
1060 MOVE -2*Ox,0
1070 FOR x=a TO b STEP inc
1080 ON ERROR LOCAL x+=inc
1090 y=EVAL(f$)
1100 DRAW 100*x,100*y
1110 NEXT x
1120 ORIGIN 0,0
1130 RESTORE ERROR
1140 ENDPROC
```

It is essential that LOCAL error be the last thing to be declared LOCAL in a procedure or function definition. The restore error as the penultimate line is included for completeness, but, as already mentioned, it is not essential here. The ON error local statement has been carefully positioned within the for...next loop. Should any error occur, the loop counter x is incremented by the code specified by ON error local, and execution then continues with the statements immediately following that one. The effect in this case is to force the loop counter on by one increment.

35

BASIC V For the Acorn Archimedes

This is satisfactory provided, of course, that the only error to occur is the "Division by zero" specifically catered for. Any other error state, such as a syntax error or pressing escape, will have unexpected consequences. The procedure will respond just as though a "Division by zero" error had occurred. One possibility is to place the local error and RESTORE ERROR instructions as brackets around the critical section of code only, but this has little aesthetic appeal and would tend to slow down execution without offering an entirely foolproof solution.

A better way might be to define an error-handling function to contain all the separate local error-handling routines. A parameter would specify which error-handling routine was required. Such a function could then cater readily for syntax errors or pressing escape, while using a function would allow a logical value to be returned which could be true if the expected error had occurred, and false otherwise. A procedure could also return a value using the return keyword. It would then be up to the host procedure to determine how to respond to this information. As.you will appreciate, once you start experimenting with local error trapping, the main problem lies in determining the sequence to be followed in the event of an error, particularly if the requirement is to continue from the point at which the error occurred Hence the reason for the position of the ON error local statement in the examples.

Here's how this approach might work cut in our plotting example:

Listing 6.3 Final plot procedure with error function.

```
1000 DBF PROCplot(Ox,Oy,inc,f$)
1010 LOCAL x,y,err%:err%=TRUE
1020 LOCAL ERROR
1030 MOVE 0,Oy:DRAW 1279,Oy
1040 MOVE Ox,1023:DRAW Ox,0
1050 ORIGIN Ox,Oy:a=-Ox/100:b=(1279-Ox)/100
1060 MOVE -2*Ox,0
1070 FOR x=a TO b STEP inc
1080 ON ERROR LOCAL err%=FNerror(1)
1090 IF err% THEN
1100 y=EVAL(f$)
1110 DRAW 100*x,100*y
1120 ELSE
1130 x=b
1140 ENDIF
1150 NEXT x
1160 ORIGIN 0,0
1170 ENDPROC
1180 :
1190 DEF FNerror(error)
```

```
1200 ON ERROR OFF
1210 LOCAL flag%:flag%=FALSE
1220 CASE error OF
1230 WHEN 1: IF ERR=18 THEN x+=inc:flag%=TRUE
1240 ENDCASE
1250 IF NOT flag% PRINT REPORT$;" at line ";ERL
1260 =flag%
```

The main procedure, PROCplot, now uses an additional local variable (err%). Initially true, this variable is assigned the value returned by FNerror in the event of any error occurring. If this is "Division by zero" then the loop continues as normal, otherwise the program forces an immediate termination of the loop and a return to the calling program.

The function, FNerror, uses a case structure which can be very easily extended during program development as further local error traps are required. Clearly, this is a much lengthier solution than our original, quite simple, local error handling, but in the development of any substantial program, this systematic approach will almost certainly prove more effective than a variety of ad hoc and overlapping local error traps.

Notice also, in the function FNerror, the use of a new pseudo-variable in BASIC V, reports. This contains a string equivalent to the error message which BASIC would display if handling errors directly.

A further change has been made to the standard error handler. This now resets @% so that any error messages and line number references are correctly formatted, but it then restores any previous setting of this variable which you may have made.

Local DATA

Under RISC OS, BASIC v allows the current data pointer to be saved to the stack and subsequently retrieved in a manner similar to that used with local error trapping. To save the current data pointer, use:

```
LOCAL DATA
```

while the previous value can be restored with:

```
RESTORE DATA
```

local data and restore data may be used anywhere within a program, but their main use is likely to be in procedure and function definitions, particularly those included in libraries. As with local error, exit from a procedure or function will automatically restore the saved data pointer. If LOCAL data is used in this way, it must be the last item declared as LOCAL within the procedure or function definition except for LOCAL ERROR, which must always be the last of all.

Thus procedure and function definitions which contain their own data statements can now avoid upsetting the data pointer in the calling program. Note, that in the procedure or function definition, using:

```
RESTORE 0+
```

will set the data pointer to the first item of data included within the procedure or function definition.

New ERROR Keyword Usage

The keyword error now has an additional function within BASIC. It allows you to specify your own error numbers and corresponding error messages. The syntax takes the form:

```
ERROR <error number>,<error message>
```

For example, we might write:

```
ERROR 999,"Too many characters in name"
```

When such a line is executed, BASIC prints a normal style error message but using the string specified. The error number given in the error statement is assigned to the pseudo-variable err. Thus the example above would produce a message:

```
Too many characters in name at line .....
```

Revised Error Numbers and Messages

The User Guide lists all the possible error numbers and corresponding error messages. Many of these have been revised or are additions for BASIC V. Note that there are many instances where several different error messages all have the same error number. BASIC chooses which error message to generate depending upon the error number and its context. Note that there are also some differences between Arthur 1.2 and RISC OS which are listed below.

   0 Line too long
   0 Incorrect in-core file description
   2 Assembler limit reached
   3 Duplicate register in multiply
   6 Type mismatch: numeric array needed
   6 Type mismatch: string array needed

BASIC V For the Acorn Archimedes

10 Arrays cannot be redimensioned
11 No room for this dim
11 No room for this dimension
11 Attempt to allocate insufficient memory
27 Missing (
37 No room for function/procedure call
42 data pointer not found on stack for restore data
48 OF missing from CASE statement
52 Can't install library
52 Bad program used as function/procedure library
52 No room for library

BASIC V For the Acorn Archimedes

7 : Matrices

BASIC V adds significant matrix handling facilities to BBC BASIC. These not only result in much shorter and simpler coding when arrays or matrices are to be manipulated in any way, but are significantly faster in operation than equivalent for...next loops. For example, initialising all the elements of a three-dimensional array is some 70 times faster in BASIC V by this method. This is indicative of how much time is spent by BASIC in repeatedly interpreting for...next instructions rather than doing useful work.

Before investigating all this new power, let's start by clarifying the use of the terms array and matrix. An array is essentially a convenient method of storing a set of data items which involves giving a name to the set as a whole and referencing each data item by its position within the set. Arrays are stored as simple lists, or as two-dimensional arrays consisting of rows and columns, or as arrays of more than two dimensions. In BASIC V, arrays may be declared to store integer or floating point numbers, or strings.

Matrices are a mathematical concept derived from a study of algebra, and are often associated with such tasks as the solution of linear simultaneous equations. A matrix is normally two-dimensional consisting of rows and columns, but may also consist of a single row or a single column. Within BASIC v, matrices are, therefore, most conveniently stored as arrays, and effectively the whole-array operations may then be used to manipulate matrices.

It is not the purpose of this book to discuss matrix operations per se, or their application, but some explanation will be included as we proceed. Matrices are essentially concerned with numbers, and in BASIC are represented by integer or floating point arrays as appropriate. However, where it makes sense, matrix operations may also be applied to string arrays. For example, adding two string arrays together will result in a new array in which each string element consists of the two original string elements, in the same positions, added or concatenated together.

When a matrix operation involves two matrices, then there are usually constraints on the numbers of rows and columns in them. In most cases, both matrices must have the same number of rows and columns, though this is not always true, and other constraints sometimes apply. These will be dealt with in relation to each matrix operation.

Furthermore, these constraints apply to the size of an array as dimensioned, and not to the number of elements currently in use. For example, although BASIC always dimensions arrays with the first element in position zero, many programmers choose to ignore this and assume that the first element is in position one. Similarly, in a general application, an array may be dimensioned for the largest case likely to arise, but in practice often holds less data, and is processed accordingly. BASIC applies matrix operation to all elements, but no problems should arise if less than all elements are in use, provided this is applied consistently. Don't ignore the zero elements in one array, use them in another, and expect a matrix operation to give a sensible answer every time!

Introducing Whole-Array Operations

In whole-array operations, arrays are referenced by giving the name followed by the opening and closing parentheses thus:

```
Total () Name$() Freq%()
```

The dim statement, as well as being used to dimension arrays, can also be used to provide information about an array previously dimensioned. By specifying the name of an array, dim will return the number of dimensions with which the array was dimensioned, while specifying the name and a dimension will give the size of that dimension. For example, if an array were dimensioned as:

```
DIM sales(20,50)
```

then:

```
DIM(sales())
```

would return the value '2';

```
DIM(sales(),1)
```

would return the value '20', and:

```
DIM(sales(),2)
```

would return the value '50'.

Used in this way, dim returns a numeric value from 1 upwards, and may be used in any situation where a numeric variable or value is acceptable. The information supplied by this use of dim is very useful if it is necessary to apply checks to matrices prior to executing any matrix operation. Perhaps its greatest benefit is in procedures and functions which may now specify arrays as parameters. A procedure definition could use dim as described above to determine both the number of dimensions and the size of each dimension of any array passed to it. This provides valuable flexibility when writing functions and procedures to manipulate arrays passed as parameters/ already covered in some detail in Chapter Five.

Whole-Array Operations: Constants

Although arrays are always initialised to zero, or to null strings, it may be necessary to assign a different value to every element in an array. This is very simple, for example:

```
data()=1    bitmap%()=FALSE  data$()=STRING$(30,CHR$32)
```

Under RISC OS it is also possible to assign different values to each element of an array by giving a list of suitable values or expressions. Thus:

```
data()=1,2,3,4,5,6,7,8, 9
```

Similarly, all the elements of an array may be incremented or decremented using the new '+=' or '-=' operators, as in:

```
data()+=1    index%()-=(inc+1)
```

The syntax here can be confusing. Where a constant value is to be assigned to all the elements of an array, it is essential that this be enclosed in parentheses if it is an expression rather than as a single value or variable. However, when incrementing or decrementing the elements of an array, parentheses are not essential. For example:

```
data ()=(inc+1)   data()+=(inc+1)  data()+=inc+1
```

are all acceptable, but:

```
data()=inc+1
```

is not. More confusingly, in the latter case the error message generated is "Type mismatch: array needed". Being aware of this will save endless frustration later. You can also copy all the elements from one array to another and negate all the elements of an array. For example:

```
New_Data()=Old_Data()    or map%()=-map%()
```

but you cannot logically negate all the elements using NOT.

Arrays: Operation on with a Constant

The next array operations to consider are those where each element of an array is to be operated on with a constant. The operations available are addition, subtraction, multiplication and division. The resulting array may then be assigned to a new array, or used to replace the elements of the original one. We can also operate on a constant with an array element, or vice versa. With addition and multiplication (both commutative) the order makes no

BASIC V For the Acorn Archimedes

difference to the result, but clearly does so with subtraction and division. Remember, each and every element will be treated in exactly the same way. Examples are:

```
data()=data()+inc     data$()=data$ ()+", "
NetPrice()=GrossPrice()*1.15
Reciprocal()"1/Integer()
```

Note the string example - any matrix operation may be used on string arrays if this makes sense. In all the above examples, where two or more arrays are involved, they must all be dimensioned the same way (ie, the same number of dimensions, and the same size for each dimension). This applies in all other examples as well, except for matrix multiplication.

Binary Operations on Arrays

The same operations of addition, subtraction, multiplication and division may be used on the corresponding elements of two arrays. Thus we could, for example, write:

```
Totals()=data1()+data2()
Profit()-Income()-Cost()
Value()"Amount()*Exchange_Rate()
Record$()=Record$()+New_Field$()
```

All these operations, including that of multiplication as specified by the '*' operator, work on corresponding pairs of elements. The resulting 'values' may then be assigned to a new array or used to replace the elements of either original array.

In addition, BASIC v also provides matrix multiplication using the '.' operator. This is quite different to the multiplication of corresponding elements as mentioned above. This mathematical operation can only be applied to two-dimensional arrays. It works as follows. The first row of the first matrix is used with the first column of the second matrix. A new element is then formed from the sum of the products of the corresponding pairs of elements. This is repeated for each row of the first matrix and each column of the second. For example:

```
    since    14 = (3*2 + 4*2)        9 = (3*-1 + 4*3)
              0 = (1*2 + -1*2)      -4 = (1*-1 + -1*3)
```

Because of the way in which matrix multiplication is definied, the number

43

BASIC V For the Acorn Archimedes

of columns of the first matrix must correspond to the number of rows of the second. Furthermore, the array to which the results of a matrix multiplication are assigned must have the same number of rows as the first matrix, and the same number of columns as the second. For any three numbers i, j, and k, the operation of matrix multiplication of the form:

```
C() = A() . B()
```

is only valid if the three arrays A, B, and C have been dimensioned as:

```
DIM A(i,j),B (j,k),C(i,k)
```

Note that for a two-dimensional array, the first subscript is the row number and the second subscript the column number. The dim statement may be used as indicated before to perform the necessary checks. For example, the matrix multiplication given above is valid only if:

```
DIM (A())=2 AND DIM (BO)=2 AND DIM (CO)=2 AND
 DIM(A(),2)=DIM(B(),1) AND
  DIM(C(),1)=DIM(A(),1) AND DIM(C0,2)=DIM(B(),2)
```

That is to say, if all three arrays have two dimensions, and that the number of columns of the first equals the number of rows of the second, and that the third array (C()) has the same number of rows as the first and the same number of columns as the second.

There are two special cases of matrix multiplication which are allowed for in BASIC v. As well as the multiplication of two two-dimensional matrices as described, a row matrix may multiply a two-dimensional matrix, and a two-dimensional matrix may multiply a column matrix, the result being a further row matrix or a further column matrix respectively. Now this could be done with two-dimensional matrices in which either i=l or k=l (referring above). However, BASIC V will also allow explicit one-dimensional arrays in this context. Thus:

```
C()=A() . B()
```

is valid if the arrays are dimensioned as:

```
DIM A(j),B(j,k),C(k)      row * matrix
```

or alternatively:

```
DIM A(i,j),B(j),C(i)      matrix * column
```

Modulus Function

RISC OS also provides a new matrix function in the form of MOD. When applied to a numeric array this returns the square root of the sum of the squares of the individual elements. Thus, for example:

```
normal()=vector()/MODvector()
```

Summation

In addition to the matrix operations described, BASIC v provides a matrix function SUM, which may be used to return the sum of all the elements in an array, or the concatenation of all elements of a string array. Therefore:

```
Total_Price = SUM(Price())
```

In the case of a string array, the elements are summed row by row from left to right, as they are for a numeric array.

Under RISC OS, BASIC v provides a second summation function, sumlen, which will return the sum of the lengths of all the strings in a string array.

General Comments

The whole-array operations provided by BASIC v are very powerful, and should be used, because of their speed of execution, in preference to any other alternatives. They also lend themselves, as you may appreciate from the examples here, to the implementation of spreadsheets and similar tasks. However, there are limitations, and once you start using arrays in this way it is easy to fall into the trap of putting them in situations for which an array is not valid. In general, you cannot create expressions involving arrays. For example:

```
Total()=(Material 0 +Labour())*1.15
```

would be rejected. Likewise, when using any of BASIC's functions you cannot substitute an array for a variable. Such statements as:

```
Record$()=STR$(data())
```

or anything similar are not allowed. The solution, in the case of the former example, is to express the statement in two separate steps:

```
Total()"Material()+Labour()
Total()=Total()*1.15
```

In the second case there is no alternative but to use an explicit for...next loop to achieve the desired result:

```
FOR I%=0 TO DIM(data(),1)
Record$(I%)=STR$(data(I%))
NEXT
```

8 : Using Colours

One of the major new features of the Archimedes is its provision of a palette of 4096 different colours. This provides an enormous choice/ particularly when compared with the six colours, plus black and white, available previously on the BBC micro. The further eight flashing colours cannot really be considered as genuinely different colours.

Of course, nothing is quite as good as it seems at first sight. The same is true of the use of colour on the Archimedes! You cannot display all 4096 colours on the screen at the same time, the maximum is 256. Furthermore, the decision by Acorn to maintain complete compatibility with the use of colour on the BBC Micro and Master series has led to additional complexity and confusion when it comes to dealing with the Archimedes.

There are two quite different approaches to the handling of colour on the Archimedes. First of all we shall look at those modes (0 to 7) used on the BBC micro, and all the other modes which allow a maximum of 16 colours on the screen at the same time. The 16 colours can be chosen to be any of the 4096 shades of colour which the Archimedes is capable of, and the methods of using and selecting these colours are similar to or an extension of those used in previous versions of BBC basic.

Modes 10,13 and 15 allow up to 256 colours to be displayed on the screen at any one time, but the method of selecting these colours is quite different to that used in the other modes. Furthermore, it is possible to choose these 256 colours to be any from the 4096 strong colour palette, but this does become quite complex, and you do not have the freedom to choose literally any colours from those available.

No. of Colours	Modes
2	0,3,4,6,18,23,25
4	1,5,8,11,19,26
16	2,7,9,12,14,16,17,20,27
256	10,13,15,21,24,28

Table 8.1 Maximum number of colours per mode.

Sixteen-Colour Modes

The same principles apply equally to 2, 4 and 16 colour modes, but where any

BASIC V For the Acorn Archimedes

examples are mode dependent, the commonly used mode 12 with a choice of 16 colours will be referred to. In each of these modes, the choice of colour in the first instance is referred to in terms of a logical colour. In mode 1, for example, these range from 0 to 3, in mode 12 from 0 to 15.

With each logical number is associated a physical colour, which is what we actually see on the screen. The corresponding default colour assignments are those which we have become accustomed to on the BBC micro (see Table 8.2).

Number	Colour	Number	Colour
0	Black	8	Flashing black/white
1	Red	9	Flashing red/cyan
2	Green	10	Flashing green/magenta
3	Yellow	11	Flashing yellow/blue
4	Blue	12	Flashing blue/yellow
5	Magenta	13	Flashing magenta/green
6	Cyan	14	Flashing cyan/red
7	White	15	Flashing white/black

Table 8.2 Default colour assignments for 16 colour modes.

At any instant of time, four colours will be active. These are the current foreground and background text colours, and the foreground and background graphics colours. With both text and graphics, the background colour is indicated by adding 128 to the logical colour number specified. This is done using colour for text and gcol for graphics.

Thus, with the default colours in mode 12:

```
COLOUR 2
```

would select green for any subsequent text, while:

```
COLOUR 128+6
```

would select cyan as the new background text colour. Using COLOUR in this way determines the foreground and background colours for any text subsequently displayed on the screen. It does not change the colours of text already displayed.

Using Colour

The position is similar with graphics, but GCOL is used instead of colour. The CCOL instruction can have one or two arguments. If a single argument is

BASIC V For the Acorn Archimedes

specified then this is the logical colour number (ie, this becomes the current graphics colour). Therefore:

```
GCOL 4
```

would select blue as the current drawing colour, while:

```
GCOL 128+3
```

would select yellow as the new graphics background colour. Remember, particularly with graphics, that selecting a new background colour does not of itself change the colour of the background. A CLS or CLG command is needed to paint a new text or graphics background, and this, of course, wipes out anything already on the screen unless text or graphics windows have been set up first.

his form of the GCOL command is new to basic V. The old form, however, is equally valid, and specifies a plotting mode as well as a colour in the form:

```
GCOL <plot action> , <logical colour>
```

Note also, that basic v has added three further variations on the plotting action to those available previously. These are quite clearly documented in the User Guide, or basic Guide (post RISC OS), under the keyword GCOL.

Changing Colours

Now that we know how to select a logical colour for text or graphics, we need to investigate how we can change the default assignment of colours and choose from the range of 4096 shades available. The principle is not new, and uses the VDU19 command to associate any physical colour with a specified logical colour. So, if we were to write:

```
VDU19,1,61
GCOL 1
```

logical colour 1 would become the current graphics colour, but the colour seen on the screen as a result would be cyan, and not the default red. This is because the vdu command has associated cyan (colour number 6) with logical colour 1. The syntax of this form of the VDU19 command is as follows:

```
VDU19,<logical colour>,<physical colour>|
```

Note the essential ' I' character at the end of the sequence. As an alternative to the use of VDU19, basic v allows the colour instruction to be used in a similar way:

```
COLOUR <logical colour>,<physical colour>
```

but without the terminating ' I' character. In this context, COLOUR has nothing to do with text colours alone. It is simply a way of linking a screen colour with a logical colour number.

One point which is important here is that any change of physical colour will affect not only any future graphics or text, but all instances of the logical colour already displayed on the screen. Changing the physical colour associated with the logical colour number used for the screen background will immediately change that background colour, but without affecting any other part of the display.

We have seen how to select a logical colour for text or graphics, and how to change the physical colour that is visible on the screen, but so far we have still been working within the 16 default colours shown in Table 8.2. How do we go about accessing the 4096 colours which the Archimedes is capable of displaying on the screen?

To do this we need to use a new variation on the VDU19 command, or the equivalent colour instruction. The syntax is:

```
VDU19,1,16,r,g,b
```

or alternatively:

```
COLOUR l,r,g,b
```

In each case, '1' is the logical colour number (range 0 to 15 for mode 12), and 'r', 'g', and 'b' represent the proportions of red, green and blue to be mixed together to achieve the desired colour. Now although these values may theoretically range from 0 to 255, colour changes only occur in steps of 16. It is sometimes better to think of the two statements in the form:

```
VDU19,1,16,16*r,16*g,16*b
```

and alternatively:

```
COLOUR 1,16*r,16*g,16*b
```

The values of 'r', 'g' and 'b' should now be in the range 0 to 15. This means a range of 16 parts red, 16 parts green and 16 parts blue, giving the total of 4096 shades (16 * 16 * 16). Using either of the above instructions you can choose any of the 16 logical colour numbers (in 16 colour modes), and set it to be any of the 4096 colours.

It is quite impractical to list all the colours which are possible even if we could agree on the correct description of each shade. Therefore, there is a comprehensive program, which is listed at the end of this chapter, for mode 12 displays. This serves two separate purposes. To start with, the main part of the program is in the form of a procedure called PROCpalette, together with a number of other supporting procedures and functions.

BASIC V For the Acorn Archimedes

The simplest way of using these procedures is to add just three lines to make a complete program (these are already included in the full listing), and run this:

```
100 MODE 12
110 PROCpalette(7)
120 END
```

The screen will show a rectangle containing the current palette. This is in the form of three small squares showing the intensities of red, green and blue, and a larger square showing the resulting mixed colour. The display also shows numerically the amounts of red, green and blue being used, in the range 0 to 15. The initial display shows brilliant white, that is determined by the '7' parameter above, made up of 16 parts red, 16 parts green and 16 parts blue.

The whole routine is mouse controlled. If you use the SELECT (left-hand) button and click on any of the three squares of red, green or blue, the intensity of the corresponding colour will be increased by one, and the composite colour will change as well, together with an updated numerical display. If you move the pointer to any position outside the display panel and click, the colour at the pointer position will be loaded into the display panel. Any subsequent changes to that colour in the panel display will be reflected wherever else it appears on the screen.

If you press the MENU (middle) button, the panel display will be replaced by a simple rectangle. Moving the mouse will move this rectangle around the screen. Pressing the MENU button again will re-display the panel in the new position. Lastly, pressing the ADJUST (right-hand) button at any time will exit from the procedure.

The routine may also be used to assist in the choice of colours in any other program. Simply append the procedures from line 1000 onwards to your program, and insert a call to PROCpalette at any suitable point. You can then experiment with your choice of colours while the display is on the screen. The routine allows the display panel to be moved around, so that you can use it while adjusting the colours in any part of your own screen display.

There are a few points to note. When PROCpalette is called, you need to specify an initial logical colour for the panel display. The routine itself sets its own palette for the logical colours 13,14 and 15. If you have used these in your own program you may find the resulting colours are changed. There is no way of avoiding this if the panel display is to show the correct proportions of red, green and blue in their true colours.

BASIC V For the Acorn Archimedes

Pointer, Border and Flashing Colours

There are four further variations on the VDU19 command for mixing colours. The command:

    VDU19,1,24,r,g,b

determines the colour for a screen border. By default the border is always black, and therefore seldom obvious. Try using this version of the VDU19 command to see the effects which can be produced. The logical colour number is of no importance here - any value will do. For example:

    VDU19,1,24,255,64,0

will produce an orange-red coloured border.

The second variation of VDU19 can be used for changing the colours of the mouse pointer. It takes the form:

    VDU19,1,25,r,g,b

The default mouse pointer uses two colours, 1 and 2. If you try:

    *POINTER
    VDU19,1,25,112,96,112
    VDU19,2,25,240,80,160

you should see a pink pointer with a grey border. You can also define your own shape of pointer, and up to three logical colours (1, 2 and 3) may be used for this purpose. The pointer colours can also be changed using the instruction:

    MOUSE COLOUR l,r,g,b

See Chapter Ten on the use of the mouse for more information on this subject.

Finally, VDU19 can also be used to set the red, green and blue proportions for flashing colours, thereby extending these to the 4096 colour palette.

The two commands are:

    VDU19,1,17,r,g,b
    VDU19,1,18,r,g,b

where the parameter '17' sets the first flash colour and '18' the second. The values 'r', 'g' and 'b' are the proportions of red, green and blue as before. The value of '1' determines which logical colour is to be set to a flashing colour pair.

Using the 256-colour modes

It is now time to look at the 256-colour modes, that is modes 10,13 and 15. The problem that arises from Acorn's decision to maintain compatibility in BASIC V with the colour control of previous versions of BBC BASIC is as follows. The colour of each pixel on the screen is stored as a byte of information in memory. Now, that would seem to be fine as one byte has a range from 0 to 255. However, a standard has already been established whereby the top bit of this byte is used to indicate whether the colour is a foreground or background colour. Setting the top bit by adding 128 to the colour number indicates a background colour. Maintaining that standard means that the remaining bits can offer a range of 0 to 128 at best. In practice not even this range is used and, as we shall see, the so-called 256- colour modes offer a choice of just 64 colours.

Using 64 Colours

In some ways, working with 64 colours is very similar to working with 16, 4 or 2 colours. The familiar instructions colour and GCOL are used to determine the current graphics or text colour, and 128 is added to this if we wish to specify a background colour. For example:

```
COLOUR 19
```

would produce pinkish-orange text, while:

```
GCOL 128+40
```

would select a rather nice grey-blue for the graphics background. To increase the range of colours from 64 up to 256, a new keyword called TINT has been added to basic. In practice tint is used to add one of four levels of white to the base colour selected by COLOUR or GCOL, thus giving a range of 256 colours.

In fact, tint can take any value in the range 0 to 256, but only four distinct ranges are recognised:

```
TINT Level 0   1     2       3
TINT Range 0-63 64-127 128-191 192-255
```

 When using TINT, keep to one set of four values, say 0, 64, 128 and 192. If no tint is specified then the default level of tint, which is zero, will always be applied. The result of this is that black, colour 0, really is black, but white, colour 63, is rather dull. To get the brightest possible white you will need to specify a tint of 192:

```
COLOUR 63 TINT 192
```

BASIC V For the Acorn Archimedes

You should be aware, though, that if you use the highest level of TINT for this reason, then the same level of TINT applied to black will result in dark grey and not true black. You should also note that the last value of TINT specified will be applied to all subsequent COLOUR and GCOL statements in the absence of any alternative specification. In general, if you wish to use TINT, use it with every colour and GCOL statement to ensure you get the required result.

Alternatively, if the same level of TINT is to be used for several colour selections, then the keyword TINT may be used on its own to achieve this. For example:

```
TINT 0,192
```

would set the highest or lightest amount of TINT for the text foreground colour. Used in this way, the first parameter of TINT specifies which colour the TINT level is to be applied to - 0 = text foreground, 1 = text background, 2 = graphics foreground, 3 = graphics background. The second parameter is the level of TINT, as before.

TINT can also be used as a function to supplement point in order to determine the colour and tint of any pixel on the screen. POINT(x,y) returns the logical colour number of the specified point, as before, while

TINT(x.y) performs a similar function but returning the level of tint at the specified point (values 0, 64, 128, or 192).

Although the default level of tint is zero, it appears that executing either *POINTER or MOUSE ON (to display the mouse pointer) has the unexpected side effect of setting the tint level to its maximum. This is an argument for getting familiar with TINT and including it in every COLOUR and GCOL statement you use.

You can use the following short program to see all 256 default colours displayed on the screen. The program works in text mode, displaying the word "COLOUR" in each shade in turn, but the same shades would apply for graphics. The BASIC colour numbers from 0 to 63 run in two columns down the screen with the colour number to the left. Each column repeats the word COLOUR four times, adding progressively more TINT from left to right. A REPEAT...UNTIL loop is used at the end of the program to maintain the finished display. Press ESCAPE to exit.

Listing 8.1 A display of 256 colours.

```
  10 REM >Chap8-1
 100 MODE 15
 110 FOR col=0 TO 63
```

53

BASIC V For the Acorn Archimedes

```
120 FOR tint=0 TO 192 STEP 64
130 COLOUR col TINT tint
140 x=-(col>31)*40:y=col+32*(col>31)
150 PRINTTAB(x,y) ;
160 IF tint=0 THEN PRINT SPC (-(col<10) ) ; STR$ (col) ;
170 PRINTTAB(x+4+tint/8,y)"COLOUR";
180 NEXT tint
190 IF col<>31 AND col<>63 THEN PRINT
200 NEXT col
210 REPEAT UNTIL FALSE
220 END
```

The program itself is fairly straightforward, but notice how the truth value of several comparisons (-1 or 0) is used to get the formatting correct. This is shown in line 140 in particular. This can be difficult to follow but is usually quite concise.

Understanding 256-Colour Modes

This chapter explains how to select any of the default 256 colours. These are, in effect, the equivalent of the logical colours we discussed with respect to other modes. However, redefining the colours to access all the 4096 shades of colour is another story altogether. To start with, it is useful to examine how the default colours are constituted.

As before, the default colours are made up from red, green and blue components, but this time a maximum of four parts of each only is allowed. This means the proportion of each colour is a number in the range 0 to 3. The actual colour number can then be computed according to the following formula

```
colour number = 16*blue + 4*green + red
```

If we treat the COLOUR number as a byte, then the bottom two bits indicate the level of red, the next two the level of green, and the next two again the level of blue. The top-most bit, of course, determines whether the colour specified is to be used for the foreground or background. If we include the level of TINT, which we have already noted offers 4 levels also, then a COLOUR (or GCOL) statement can be expressed as:

```
COLOUR 16*blue+4*green+red TINT 64*tint
```

where each of blue, green, red and tint is in the range 0 to 3.

Redefining the Palette

Broadly, the way in which physical colours are linked to logical colour numbers, is through the use of a set of 16 palette registers. The register defines the actual colour to be used, while the logical colour number acts as an index to a palette register.

In those modes using 16 or fewer colours this all works beautifully as there is no problem in assigning one palette register to each logical number. By default the palette registers are set up with the colours as listed in Table 8.2. To display the correct colour at any point on the screen, which is constantly refreshed by information from the computer, the corresponding memory byte acts as an index to a palette register. The contents of the palette register control the output to the red, green and blue guns of the monitor. With 16 different levels to each of three colours - that makes four bits times three, making 12 bits in all.

The problem that arises in modes 10,13 and 15 is, of course, that we have only 16 registers to cope with the demands of 64 logical colours plus the four levels of TINT. The mechanism which is used is not simple, and attempting to change the palette in these modes can easily produce unexpected, and maybe undesirable, results.

In essence it works like this. The four levels of red, green and blue each supply two bits, which together with the four levels of TINT, again two bits, makes up a colour value of eight bits, which is stored in screen memory. From this, in conjunction with the palette registers, we need to form 12 bits to send to the monitor. The top four bits of the memory byte (1 bit red, 2 bits green, 1 bit blue) are sent directly to the screen D to A converters. The bottom four bits (range 0 to 15) form an index into a palette register which then supplies the remaining eight bits of colour information (3 bits red, 2 bits green, 3 bits blue).

The default palette settings in these modes have been carefully designed so that tint has the effect described, of adding one of four levels of white to any of 64 BASIC colours. If any of the palette settings are changed, this relationship is completely destroyed. Furthermore, changing a palette register definition affects not just one but sixteen of the BASIC colours. Redefining a palette register to change one colour to the desired subtle shade is likely to ensure that the other 15 colours affected change to shades that are less than useful. All of this is a recipe for potential disaster, and most programmers would do well to leave everything as it is. The default 256 colours have been carefully selected by Acorn to give a good range of colours.

The third program in this chapter demonstrates how to redefine the palette registers in order to display successively all of the Archimedes possible 4096 colours in a 256-colour mode (mode 15). The program displays the colours 16 at a time, each colour corresponding to the re- definition of a different palette register.

The 4096 colours can, in essence, be generated by cycling through 16 levels of

BASIC V For the Acorn Archimedes

red, green and blue, and three nested FOR...NEXT loops in the program do just that. Lines 220 to 240 determine the top four bits of the colour number (bit 3 blue, bits 2 and 3 green, and bit 3 red). These can then be combined to form (at line 250) a first approximation to the colour number for the following GCOL statement. This is further refined so that each level of blue cycled through specifies a different palette register. The contents of the corresponding palette register are set to the correct levels of red, green and blue by our old friend the VDU19 command at line 260. The last point to note is that the full specification of which palette register to use is determined partly by the GCOL number (bits 4 and 0) and partly by the shifted TINT value. Any previous concept of the latter's use as a TINT has quite disappeared.

Listing 8.2 Palette redefinition in 256 colour modes

```
 10 REM >Chap8-2
100 MODE 15:OFF:ON ERROR MODE12:END
110 x=480:y=846:w=128:h=128
120 xl=0:yl=6:wl=7:hl=2
130 COLOUR 30
140 PRINTTAB(28,2)"4096 COLOURS in MODE 15"
150 PRINTTAB(26,3)"(using 16 palette registers)"
160 PRINTTAB (14,30)"Press SPACE BAR for the next 16-colour set;"
170 PRINTTAB(22,31)"Hold down SHIFT to jump 16 sets."
180 PRINTTAB(xl+9,yl)"Colour Set"
185 PRINTTAB(xl+9,yl+12)"GCOL/TINT"
190 FOR red%=0 TO 15
200 FOR green%=0 TO 15
210 FOR blue%=0 TO 15
220 blue3%=(bluet AND %1000)>>2
230 green23%=(green% AND %1100)>>2
240 red3%=(red% AND %1000)>>2
250 col%=(blue3%<<4) + (green23%<<2) + (red3%)
260 VDU19, bluet, 16, red%«4, green%«4,blue%«4
270 col%=col%-1*(blue%DIV4=1 OR blue%DIV4=3)-16*(blue%DIV4=2 OR blue%DIV4=3)
280 tint%=(blue%MOD4)<<6
290 GCOL col% TINT tint's
300 RECTANGLEFILL (x+1.5*w*(blue%MOD4)),(y-1.5*h*(blue%DIV4)-h),w,h
310 PRINTTAB(x/16+1.5*w/16*(blue%MOD4)+2,32-y/32+(1,5*h*(blue%DIV4)+h+32)/32)"p";STR$(bluet)
320 PRINTTAB(xl+wl*(blue%MOD4),yl+hl*(blue%DIV4)+2)STR$(256*rd%+16*green%+blue%);SPC3;
325 PRINTTAB(xl+wl*(blue%MOD4),yl+12+hl*(blue%DIV4)+2)STR$(col%;" ";STR$(tint%);SPC3
```

BASIC V For the Acorn Archimedes

```
 330 NEXT blue%:G=GET:IF INKEY-1 THEN red%-=red%<15
 340 NEXT green%:NEXT red%
 350 REPEAT UNTIL FALSE
 360 END
```

You can cycle through all 4096 colours by pressing the space bar to control the display. The GCOL and TINT values for each colour are also shown on the screen. On a technical point, note the frequent use of the '>>>' and '<<' operators for multiplying and dividing by two, much the quickest way of achieving this. Thus the value after tint% at line 280 is given as (blue%MOD4)<<6 where the '<<6' is the same as multiplying by 2 a total of six times (ie, a value of 64).

As a final point, VDU19 can still be used as described for the other modes to change the pointer and screen border colours. They are selected by specifying the proportions of red, green and blue in the usual way.

Final Comments

While the large range of colours is certainly one of the major features of the Archimedes, the control and selection of colours is also more complex than hitherto. However, the potential is enormous and there must be a multitude of exciting visual effects just waiting to be discovered. All that is needed is a little imagination along with a good deal of time and effort.

Listing 8.3 Mode 12 palette display

```
   10 REM >Chap8-3
  100 MODE12
  110 PROCpalette(7)
  120 END
  130 :
 1000 DEF PROCpalette(pixel)
 1010 LOCAL x,y,z,bx,by,w,h,exit%,r,g,b
 1020 w=256:h=224:exit%=FALSE
 1030 r=15:g=15:b=15
 1040 bx=512:by=384
 1050 *POINTER
 1060 MOUSE TO bx,by
 1070 PROCselect_colour(0,0,bx,by,FALSE)
 1080 PROCshow_palette(bx,by)
 1090 REPEAT
 1100 MOUSE x,y,z
 1110 CASE z OF
 1120 WHEN 1:exit%=TRUE
```

BASIC V For the Acorn Archimedes

```
1130 WHEN 2:PROCmove_palette(x,y,bx,by)
1140 WHEN 4:PROCpick(x,y,bx,by)
1150 ENDCASE
1160 TIME=0:REPEAT UNTIL TIME>8
1170 UNTIL exit%
1180 *SCHOOSE palette
1190 PLOT &ED,bx-4,by-8
1200 MOUSE OFF
1210 ENDPROC
1220 :
1230 DEF PROCshow_palette(x,y)
1240 MOVE x-4,y-8:MOVEx+w+4,y+h+8
1250 *SGET palette
1260 PROCset_colours
1270 PROCdraw_frame(x,y)
1280 PROCshow_colours(x,y)
1290 PROCwrite_text(x,y)
1300 PROCwrite_numbers(x,y)
1310 ENDPROC
1320 :
1330 DEF PROCdraw_frame(x,y)
1340 GCOL 12:RECTANGLE FILLx,y,w,h
1350 GCOL 7
1360 RECTANGLE x,y,w,h
1370 RECTANGLE x-4,y-8,w+8,h+16
1380 GCOL 0
1390 RECTANGLE x-2,y-4,w+4,h+8
1400 ENDPROC
1410 :
1420 DEF PROCshow_colours(x,y)
1430 LOCAL colour
1440 FOR colour=1 TO 3
1450 GCOL colour+12
1460 RECTANGLE FILL x+1 6+80*(colour.-1) , y+h-104, 64, 64
1470 NEXT colour
1480 GCOL pixel
1490 RECTANGLE FILL x+16,y+16,w-32,64
1500 ENDPROC
1510 :
1520 DEF PROCwrite_text(x,y)
1530 GCOL 7:VDU5
1540 MOVE x+24,y+h-8:PRINT"Red"
1550 MOVE x+88,y+h-8:PRINT"Green"
1560 MOVE x+176,y+h-8:PRINT"Blue"
1570 VDU4
1580 ENDPROC
1590 :
1600 DEF PROCwrite_numbers(x,y)
```

```
1610 GCOL 12:RECTANGLE FILL x+16,y+80,224,32
1620 GCOL 7:VDU5
1630 MOVE x+30, y+112 :PRINT FNjustd-,2)
1640 MOVE x+110,y+112:PRINT FNjust(g,2)
1650 MOVE x+190,y+112:PRINT FNjust(b,2)
1660 VDU4
1670 ENDPROC
1680 :
1690 DEF FNjust(v,f)
1700 LOCAL v$:v$=STR$(v)
1710 =STRING$(f-LEM(v$)," ")+v
1720 :
1730 DEF PROCmove_palette(x,y,RETURN bx,RETURN by)
1740 LOCAL z,exit%:exit%=FALSE
1750 *SCHOOSE palette
1760 PLOT &ED,bx-4,by-8
1770 MOUSE TO x,y
1780 MOUSE RECTANGLE 4,8,1279-W-8,1023-h-16
1790 GCOL 3,6
1800 REPEAT:MOUSE x,y,z:UNTIL z=0
1810 REPEAT
1820 MOUSE x,y,z
1830 RECTANGLE x,y,w,h
1840 IF z=2 THEN
1850 RECTANGLE x,y,w,h
1860 PROCshow_palette(x,y)
1870 exit%=TRUE:bx=x:by=y
1880 REPEAT:MOUSE x,y,z:UNTIL z=0
1890 ELSE
1900 WAIT
1910 RECTANGLE x,y,w,h
1920 ENDIF
1930 UNTIL exit%
1940 MOUSE RECTANGLE 0,0,1279,1023
1950 ENDPROC
1960 :
1970 DEF FNarea(x,y,xl,yl,w,h)=(x>=xl AND x<=xl+w AND y>=yl AND
y<=yl+h)
1980 :
1990 DEF PROCpick(x,y,bx,by)
2000 CASE TRUE OF
2010 WHEN NOT FNarea(x,y,bx,by,w,h):PROCselect_
colour(x,y,bx,by,TRUE)
2020 WHEN FNarea(x,y,bx+16,by+h-112,64,64):PROCchange_colour(r)
2030 WHEN FNarea(x,y,bx+96,by+h-112,64,64):PROCchange_colour(g)
2040 WHEN FNarea(x,y,bx+176,by+h-112,64,64):PROCchange_
colour(b)
2050 ENDCASE
```

BASIC V For the Acorn Archimedes

```
2060 PROCupdate_palette
2070 ENDPROC
2080 :
2090 DEF PROCselect_colour(x,y,bx,by,flag%)
2100 LOCAL p1,p2
2110 IF flag% THEN pixel=POINT(x,y)
2120 SYS "OS_ReadPalette",pixel,16 TO ,,p1,p2
2130 r=p1>>>12 AND &FF
2140 g=p1>>>20 AND &FF
2150 b=p1>>>28
2160 IF flag% PROCshow_colours(bx,by)
2170 ENDPROC
2180 :
2190 DEF PROCchange_colour(RETURN c)
2200 c=(c+1)MOD16
2210 ENDPROC
2220 :
2230 DEF PROCset_colours
2240 COLOUR 13,16*r,0,0
2250 COLOUR 14,0,16*g,0
2260 COLOUR 15,0,0,16*b
2270 COLOUR pixel,16*r,16*g,16*b
2280 COLOUR 12,0,0,0
2290 ENDPROC
2300 :
2310 DEF PROCupdate_palette
2320 PROCset_colours
2330 PROCwrite_numbers(bx,by)
2340 ENDPROC
```

BASIC V For the Acorn Archimedes

9 : Graphics

The original BBC Micro was relatively well endowed with graphics capabilities when it was launched in 1981, and for BASIC programmers this was reflected in specific keywords, particularly plot, and the variety of so-called vdu commands. The later 1.2 Operating System increased the scope of the plot function, and the graphics capabilities of the BBC Micro were further extended with Acorn's Graphics Extension rom, the features of which were subsequently built into the Operating System used on the Master 128 and Master Compact.

Unfortunately, no additional support has been provided explicitly within BASIC for any of these new features until the advent of BASIC V on the Archimedes. Instead, everything new had had to be handled through the use of plot and vdu instructions.

Of course, many graphics functions are significantly faster on an Archimedes, but the system as a whole incorporates only a few additional functions, plotting sprites for example. However, many more graphics functions now have an associated BASIC keyword, which both tends to draw attention to features which might otherwise be overlooked, as well as making such features easier to use for many Archimedes owners. There is one major change as far as graphics is concerned, and that is in the availability of the range of colours and modes supporting up to 256 different colours on the screen together. This important, but sometimes complex, subject was dealt with in the preceding chapter.

New Graphics Commands

The new BASIC instructions can be listed as follows:

```
CIRCLE       CIRCLE FILL
ELLIPSE      ELLIPSE FILL
RECTANGLE    RECTANGLE FILL
LINE
FILL         FILL BY
ORIGIN
POINT        POINT BY      POINT TO
MOVE BY      DRAW BY
```

The ORIGIN instruction duplicates the VDU29 command by allowing the origin for graphics to be moved to a new position. As with all BASIC instructions which package up VDU commands, the two arguments, the x and

61

BASIC V For the Acorn Archimedes

y co-ordinates, are separated by a simple comma instead of the semi- colons needed to terminate values in excess of 255 in VDU commands. So:

```
ORIGIN 640,512
```

would move the origin to the centre of the screen. When specifying a new origin, the co-ordinates of the position are always given relative to an origin at the bottom left-hand corner of the screen. Similarly, the point instruction duplicates, for convenience, one of the plot commands, PLOT69, to allow a point to be plotted at a specified position. Therefore:

```
POINT 640,512
```

will plot a point at the centre of the screen, assuming the origin in its default position, and:

```
POINT BY 640,512
```

will also plot a point but by moving 640 units horizontally and 512 points vertically relative to the previous screen position. This variation duplicates the PLOT61 command. The POINT command adds no new function to BASIC V, but is an example where the use of an alternative and more meaningful BASIC keyword will help beginners to master graphics.

The POINT TO instruction may be used to move the screen pointer when this is not under mouse control. See Chapter Ten for information on using the MOUSE ON instruction. The pointer will be moved to the screen position specified, for example:

```
POINT TO 160, 128
```

The LINE instruction is a different kind of convenience in that it does not duplicate any individual PLOT or VDU command but provides a single instruction for what previously required two. Thus:

```
MOVE x1,y1
DRAW x2,y2
```

can now be written as:

```
LINE x1,y1,x2,y2
```

in order to draw a line from one point (x1,y1) to another (x2,y2). The three new shape drawing instructions, however, are again BASIC keywords duplicating existing plot instructions (on the Master 128 and Compact), and simplifying the specification of size and position into the bargain. All three instructions produce an outline shape, or a filled shape if the keyword FILL is included. The CIRCLE instruction is of the form:

```
CIRCLE x,y,r
```

where x/y is the centre of the circle, and r is the radius. The Ellipse drawing function has the format:

```
ELLIPSE x,y,m1,m2
```

where x,y is the centre as before, m1 is the length of the semi-major axis, and m2 is the length of the semi-minor axis. A fifth parameter may also be included which, if present, specifies the angle in radians between the x axis and the semi-major axis. For example:

```
ELLIPSE FILL 640,512,100,75,PI/2
```

would draw a filled ellipse at the centre of the screen (assuming a default origin), with major axis 200 units and minor axis 150 units rotated through 90 degrees into a vertical position. The statement is equivalent to:

```
ELLIPSE FILL 640,512,75,100
```

by reversing the lengths of the semi-major and semi-minor axes. Note that there are some limits imposed on the parameters to the ellipse instruction if an error is not to be generated. This is covered quite clearly in the User Guide (look up ELLIPSE).

The RECTANGLE statement is the last of the new BASIC keywords for drawing shapes and, as well as the FILL variation, may take either four or six parameters. In its simplest form, the first two parameters specify the co-ordinates of one corner, while the other two, which may be positive or negative, specify offsets horizontally and vertically from the first corner to the opposite corner. For example:

```
RECTANGLE FILL 480,384,320,256
```

would display a solid rectangle in the current graphics foreground colour at the centre of the screen. Note that when an outline rectangle is drawn, the graphics cursor remains at the first reference point, but that when a filled rectangle is displayed the graphics cursor is left at the opposite corner. This is exactly what would be expected if a rectangle were to be explicitly drawn as a sequence of four straight lines or two filled triangles, using MOVE and DRAW or PLOT, as with previous versions of BBC BASIC.

A second form of the RECTANGLE (or RECTANGLE FILL) statement requires two further parameters and allows the rectangular area of the screen, defined as before by the first four parameters, to be copied (no FILL) or moved (FILL) to a new position on the screen. Any graphics image contained within the rectangle defined will be copied or moved as a result, providing a 'copy and paste' or 'cut and paste' facility for graphics. When an image is to be moved, its original area is filled with the current graphics background colour.

The following program uses the same procedure, PROCrectangle, as Chapter Ten to demonstrate the use of the 'copy and paste' facility described above. The program fills the screen with randomly sized and coloured ellipses. The

BASIC V For the Acorn Archimedes

mouse may then be used to select any rectangular area of the screen and copy its contents elsewhere. Used in a continuous manner, it produces a 'painting' effect with attractive results.

Listing 9.1 Graphics demonstration.

```
   10 REM >Chap9-1
  100 MODE12:OFF
  105 ON ERROR MODE12:PRINT REPORT$;" at line ";ERL:END
  110 PROCellipses
  120 xl=320:yl=256:w=160:h=128
  130 PROCrectangle(4,xl,yl,w,h)
  140 MOUSE RECTANGLE 0,0,1279-w,1023-h
  150 MOUSE TO 160,128
  160 REPEAT
  170 MOUSE x,y,z
  180 PROCcopy(xl,yl,w,h,x,y)
  190 UNTIL FALSE
  200 END
  210 :
 1000 DEF PROCrectangle(colour,RETURN xl,RETURN yl,RETURN w,RETURN h)
 1010 LOCAL exit's, switch's, x, y : GCOL 3,colour
 1020 *POINTER
 1030 exit%=FALSE:switch%=TRUE
 1040 MOUSE TO xl,yl
 1060 REPEAT
 1070 RECTANGLE xl,yl,w,h
 1080 MOUSE x,y, z
 1090 IF z THEN
 1100 CASE z OF
 1110 WHEN 4:switch%=NOT switch%'
 1120 IF switch% THEN MOUSE TO xl,yl ELSE MOUSE TO x+w,y+h
 1130 WHEN 1: exit%=TRUE
 1140 ENDCASE
 1150 REPEAT:MOUSE x,y,z:UNTIL z=0
 1160 ENDIF
 1170 WAIT
 1180 RECTANGLE xl,yl,w,h
 1190 IF switch% THEN xl=x:yl=y ELSE w=x-xl:h=y-yl
 1200 UNTIL exit%
 1210 *POINTER 0
 1220 ENDPROC
 1230 :
 1240 DEF PROCellipses
 1250 LOCAL n
 1260 FOR n=1 TO 100
```

BASIC V For the Acorn Archimedes

```
1270 GCOL RND(8)-1
1280 ELLIPSE FILL RND (1100)+100,RND(900)+100,RND(100)+100,R
ND(100)+100
1290 NEXT n
1300 ENDPROC
1310 :
1320 DEF PROCcopy(RETURN x1,RETURN y1,RETURN w,RETURN h,x2,y2)
1330 RECTANGLE x1,y1,w,h TO x2,y2
1340 x1=x2:y1=y2
1350 ENDPROC
```

Use the mouse to move the rectangle around the screen. Pressing the SELECT button fixes the position but allows the size and proportions to be changed. You can swap between these two adjustments until you are happy with the area selected. Pressing the ADJUST button then turns that area into a paint brush for painting on the screen. Just move the mouse around to produce spectacular effects.

The program uses two further procedures, PROCellipses and PROCcopy. The former simply calls the ELLIPSE FILL instruction 100 times, specifying randomly selected values for the position and shape in each case. PROCrectangle is then called to allow the user to define a rectangular area of this display. Finally PROCcopy is called repeatedly to copy the image area defined to a new position determined by the movement of the mouse. Line 140 ensures that the image area always remains on-screen by restricting the movement of the mouse, while line 150 displays the image area in a convenient but arbitrary starting position. In the definition of PROCcopy, note the use of return with the first four parameters, so that each new position is remembered and used as the starting point of the next move or copy which is carried out by the RECTANGLE statement at line 1330. If you try this program out, as well as demonstrating the use of a good many of the new features of BASIC V, you will also end up with some highly colourful and attractive displays.

Fill Routines

The new fill instruction allows any area of the screen to be flood-filled using the current foreground colour. The instruction requires just two parameters which specify the x,y co-ordinates of the starting point for the fill. The only other requirement is that the starting point must match the currently selected background colour, otherwise nothing happens. This problem can be easily avoided by using the following sequence. Assume the current foreground and background colours are always held in the variables fc and bc respectively. A suitable routine could be written as:

BASIC V For the Acorn Archimedes

```
MOVE x,y
bc=POINT(x,y)
GCOL be + 128: FILL x,y
```

The background is set to the colour at the point from which the fill will take place before the FILL instruction is executed. The instruction then fills in all directions until a non-background colour, the edge of the screen or the edge of the graphics window, is reached. The variation FILL BY performs exactly the same function as the FILL instruction above, except that the co-ordinates for the starting point are taken to be relative to the last position of the graphics cursor rather than being absolute co- ordinates. Whichever format is used, a flood-fill on the Archimedes is very fast indeed.

Relative Co-ordinates

We have already seen how the incorporation of 'BY' in two keywords (POINT BY and FILL BY) allows a point to be specified relative to the last position of the graphics cursor, rather than in absolute terms. This use of by can also be applied to the two instructions MOVE and DRAW in exactly the same way.

Plotting Sprites

The Archimedes provides support for sprites with a number of star commands and additions to the range of PLOT functions in BASIC, in addition to the sprite editor supplied on the Welcome disc. The star commands are, of course, not part of basic but access the SpriteUtils system module. These commands are listed here for reference:

Command	Description
*SCHOOSE	selects a sprite by name for plotting
*SCOPY	makes a copy of a sprite
*SCREENLOAD	plots a sprite directly from a file to screen
*SCREENSAVE	saves the current graphics window as a sprite
*SDELETE	deletes one or more sprites from memory
*SFLIPX	reflects a sprite about the x axis
*SFLIPY	reflects a sprite about the y axis
*SGET	saves a rectangular area of the screen as a sprite
*SINFO	displays information on the sprite workspace
*SLIST	lists the sprites currently in memory
*SLOAD	loads a file of sprite definitions into memory
*SMERGE	merges two sets of sprite definitions
*SNEW	clears the sprite workspace
*SRENAME	renames a sprite

*SSAVE   save all sprites currently in memory

The currently selected sprite may be plotted at any point on the screen by using a plot instruction (PLOT232 - PLOT239). The different values have the usual range of meanings for plot commands. For example:

```
PLOT &ED,640,512
```

would plot the currently selected sprite at the centre of the screen, assuming the default position for the origin. This is the most likely plotting mode to be used, often in conjunction with Exclusive OR plotting to achieve apparent movement on the screen. Of particular interest, *SGET allows any rectangular area of the screen to be saved as a sprite. *SCHOOSE selects any sprite in memory ready for plotting on the screen using PLOT&ED. These commands were used to good effect in the final program of Chapter Eight (listing 8.3).

Sprites are covered in detail in the User Guide for BASIC programmers, and in the Programmer's Reference Manual for those who require more detailed information.

10 : Archimedes Mouse

The Archimedes is supplied with a three-button mouse as standard, and this device is fully supported by extensions to BBC BASIC. Acorn has recommended that software writers follow the convention that the left- hand button is designated SELECT, the middle button MENU, and the right-hand button ADJUST. However, this convention is not imposed upon the programmer, who can alternatively choose to associate each button with any function appropriate to his program. BASIC V provides instructions to enable and disable the mouse and, when enabled, to return to a program the state of the three buttons and the graphics co-ordinates of its current position.

A pointer can also be displayed such that moving the mouse automatically moves the pointer within any rectangular screen area defined by the user's program. The default is the whole screen area. The default pointer shape is an upward-sloping blue arrow, but it is possible for a user- defined pointer shape to be used instead, and up to four different pointer designs may be valid concurrently, with the ability for a program to select which pointer to display. However, the design of a pointer shape involves setting up a data block in memory and using a system call to the Wimp manager, a task which is outside the immediate scope of this book. Note that because the mouse pointer is controlled by the Wimp manager, removing or deleting this module will make it impossible for any pointer to be displayed.

Whether the default or a user defined pointer shape is used, the size and proportions of the pointer displayed will, like text, depend upon the screen mode in use. If you want a pointer to appear exactly the same in a 40-column mode and an 80-column mode, then one solution would be to define two pointer shapes to proportions which will exactly compensate for any distortions introduced by the characteristics of the different modes.

Whatever pointer shape is used, BASIC provides the means of varying its colours regardless of how these were originally defined.

The first command to consider is not in fact a BASIC instruction at all, but a call to the Wimp manager, in the form:

```
*POINTER <n>
```

This enables the pointer to be used with the mouse. The single value parameter is optional. If no parameter is specified then the default system defined pointer is displayed. A parameter of '1' also selects the default pointer, while other values select user-defined pointers. A parameter of '0' disables the pointer. Once *POINTER has been executed, a pointer can be switched on and off with one of BASIC's MOUSE instructions. Thus, using:

```
MOUSE ON
```

will display the default pointer, while an instruction of the form:

```
MOUSE ON n
```

will display pointer 'n' with the same values and meanings as above for "pointer. However, unlike "pointer, 'n' may be either a value or an expression in this case, giving more flexibility in the use of this instruction.

To switch a pointer off simply use:

```
MOUSE OFF
```

Note that changing mode will also cause the pointer to disappear from the screen, but MOUSE ON, with or without a parameter as required, is sufficient to restore it.

There is a further variation of the MOUSE ON command which is undocumented in the User Guide. If 128 is added to the pointer number (n), the pointer is enabled (ie, it appears on the screen) as described above, but is 'disconnected' from the mouse. Once this has been done, the pointer may be moved to any location using the POINT TO command to specify a point in graphics units on the screen. The only oblique reference in the User Guide is in connection with "FX106 which is entirely equivalent to MOUSE ON. Using MOUSE ON with a pointer number less than 129 will restore mouse control, while MOUSE OFF will remove the pointer altogether.

Input from the Mouse

A single instruction is provided by basic to return the position of the mouse and the state of the mouse buttons. You need to include three variables such as x, y, and z as shown here. The instruction takes the form:

```
MOUSE x,y,z
```

where x and y are the graphics co-ordinates of the active point of the pointer, and z indicates which buttons, if any, are depressed at that time. It is simplest to think of the three buttons as three binary switches with values of 0 (off) and 1 (on or depressed). Combining the resulting three bits gives a number in the range 0 to 7, where a value of 0 indicates all three buttons are 'off, and a value of 7 that all three buttons are 'on'. Operated individually, the adjust button (the right one) returns '1' (binary 001), the menu button (in the middle) returns '2' (binary 010), while the select button (to the left) returns '4' (binary 100).

In use, this instruction will normally be placed at the start of a loop which is executed repeatedly. In most cases, either the button or combination of buttons pressed, or the position of the pointer on the screen, will determine any action

BASIC V For the Acorn Archimedes

to be taken. Typically a CASE statement is the best choice for handling this situation. Consider, for example:

```
exit%=FALSE
REPEAT
MOUSE xpos,ypos,state
CASE state OF
  WHEN 7:exit%=TRUE
  WHEN 4:PROCselect(xpos,ypos)
  WHEN 2:PROCmenu(xpos,ypos)
  WHEN 1:PROCadjust(xpos,ypos)
ENDCASE
UNTIL exit%
```

This responds to any of the three buttons being pressed individually by calling a corresponding procedure, while pressing all three buttons together causes an exit from the loop. An alternative approach, making use of the pointer position, might be written as:

```
exit%=FALSE
REPEAT
MOUSE x,y,buttons
CASE TRUE OF
  WHEN FNpos(x,y,a1,b1,width,height):PROCmenu(1,buttons)
  WHEN FNpos (x,y,a2,b2,width,height):PROCmenu(2,buttons)
  WHEN FNpos(x,y,a3,b3,width,height):PROCmenu(3,buttons)
  WHEN FNpos(x,y,a9,b9,width,height):exit%=TRUE
ENDCASE
UNTIL exit%
```

This routine assumes the existence of a function (FNpos) which checks whether the current pointer position lies within a specified screen rectangle defined by the co-ordinates of its bottom left-hand corner, width and height, and returns a value of true or false depending on the result. This would suit a situation where a number of menu options were displayed in boxes on the screen. The routine above calls a menu procedure in each case, passing the number of the menu option specified, and the button status.

Both approaches can be combined together. Typically, the select button would be used to pick out a menu choice displayed on the screen, with the other buttons having no effect. An additional CASE OF statement will do the job as follows:

```
 exit%=FALSE
 REPEAT
  MOUSE x,y,buttons
  CASE buttons OF
   WHEN 4:
    CASE TRUE OF
```

70

```
      WHEN FNpos(x,y,a1,b1,width,height):PROCmenu(1)
      WHEN FNpos(x,y,a2,b2,width,height):PROCmenu(2)
      WHEN FNpos(x,y,a3,b3,width,height):PROCmenu(3)
      WHEN FNpos(x,y,a9,b9,width,height):exit%=TRUE
    ENDCASE
  ENDCASE
UNTIL exit%
```

An if...then...endif structure could be used as an alternative to the outer- most CASE statement - your choice will depend on just what the code is trying to achieve.

One of the problems that can only too easily arise when using the mouse, is that the button is depressed for too long, resulting in several sets of values (for x, y and z) ending up in the mouse buffer. The sheer speed of the Archimedes itself exacerbates this problem. The best way of avoiding this is to use a REPEAT...UNTIL loop to check that all the buttons have been released before checking for the next mouse input, and then a second loop to wait for a button press:

```
REPEAT
REPEAT:Mouse x,y,z:UNTIL z=0
REPEAT:MOUSE x,y,z:UNTIL z<>0
........
UNTIL exit%
```

Further Mouse Controls

When the Archimedes is first switched on, or after a mode change, the selected pointer is displayed at the centre of the screen (ie, the MOUSE x,y,z instruction would return x=640, y=512). Otherwise, if MOUSE ON and MOUSE OFF are used to switch pointers on and off, the pointer always appears in the last pointer position. A program can alternatively ensure that the pointer is displayed in a particular position by using the instruction:

```
MOUSE TO x,y
```

where x and y are in graphics co-ordinates. A program can also limit the area of the screen over which the pointer may be moved with the instruction:

```
MOUSE RECTANGLE x,y,w,h
```

where x and y are the co-ordinates of the bottom left-hand corner, and w and h are the width and height respectively, of the area concerned. This can be useful if the mouse is being used to move an object round the screen, to ensure that the whole of the object remains on-screen at all times. Note that limiting the position of the pointer in this way is quite independent of any text or graphics

BASIC V For the Acorn Archimedes

windows which you may create at the same time. Changing mode restores the pointer area to the full screen display.

A further instruction may be used to control the speed of movement of the pointer on the screen in relation to the movement of the mouse itself. Another way of looking at this is in terms of the physical distance the mouse has to move to cover the full screen width or height. The instruction takes the format:

```
MOUSE STEP xstep,ystep
```

where 'xstep' and 'ystep' can be thought of as multipliers controlling horizontal and vertical movement respectively. The second parameter is optional, in which case both are set to the same value. The default values are both 1. Changing both the x and y multipliers to 2 will double the speed of movement and result in the mouse having to be moved only half the previous distance to obtain full screen movement. If non-integers are used the values will be truncated to integer values. Hence values less than 1 all truncate to zero, resulting in no mouse movement whatsoever. Using negative values will cause the screen pointer to move in the opposite direction to that of the mouse itself!

Colouring the Mouse Pointer

All pointers are defined within a rectangular area, and may use up to three colours, logically colours 1, 2 and 3. Logical colour 0 represents the transparent parts of the pointer design, where the screen display is not obscured, and may not be changed, but any of the Archimedes 4096 colours may be assigned to the pointer's three logical colours. There are two equivalent ways of doing this using either:

```
MOUSE COLOUR l,r,g,b
```

or:

```
VDU19,25,1,r,g,b
```

The logical colour 1 may be set to 1, 2 or 3 (higher values simply repeat values 0 to 3), while the values r, g, and b specify the amounts of red, green and blue (each in the range 0 to 255) to be mixed to obtain the required colour. The values specified follow the rules so that the values of r, g and b only change meaningfully in steps of 16. Both forms of the instruction may be better written as:

```
MOUSE COLOUR 1,16«r, '- 6*g,16*b
```

or:

```
VDU19,1,25,16*r,16*g,16*b
```

BASIC V For the Acorn Archimedes

where r, g and b are integers in the range 0 to 15. When selecting or changing the colours for a pointer, it is important to take into account the other colours on the screen to avoid the pointer becoming invisible. The default pointer shape with its coloured border ensures that the pointer remains visible even when placed over areas of colour which are the same as those used in the pointer itself. You can also change the default pointer to have a more solid appearance by making both the inside and the border the same shade, provided that that shade is not used elsewhere on the active screen area. The whole subject of colour on the Archimedes is explained in detail in Chapter Eight.

Switching pointers on and off with the MOUSE ON and MOUSE OFF instructions retains the current colour assignments for any pointer, but using *POINTER to delete and then display a pointer will result in the use of the colours in the original definition (dark and light blue for the default pointer). Mode changes also leave the pointer colours unchanged.

Example Mouse Program

We will now consider an extended example, in the form of a complete program, which illustrates the use of the mouse and the new RECTANGLE graphics statement. The whole routine has been written as a procedure, to make it easy to incorporate into other programs, with a short demonstration of what it does. Initially, the procedure displays a rectangle on the screen. As the mouse is moved around, so the rectangle moves. Pressing the select button fixes the bottom left-hand corner while allowing the opposite corner to be moved to change the proportions and size of the rectangle displayed. Pressing select fixes the size, and once more allows the rectangle to be moved as a whole. Both position and size can be repeatedly changed until the adjust button is pressed, whereupon the procedure exits, returning the x,y co-ordinates, width and height of the resulting rectangle. The short demo program accompanying the procedure displays these values and the rectangle on the screen.

The complete program, including the procedure PROCrectangle, is listed below. The procedure requires five parameters, the first being the logical colour to be used for the rectangle, and the other four the x,y co-ordinates of a corner and the width and height of the rectangle. When the procedure is called, these last four parameters should be used to determine the initial position and size of the rectangle to be displayed. On exit they return the final values of the same parameters.

Within the procedure, the main loop runs from lines 1060 to 1200. This is a REPEAT...UNTIL loop which constantly checks the mouse and maintains and

BASIC V For the Acorn Archimedes

changes the rectangle displayed on the screen until the adjust button exits from the loop and, ultimately, the procedure. Exclusive OR plotting is used with the RECTANGLE statement to repeatedly draw and erase the rectangle, while either the reference co-ordinates, or the width and height, are updated accordingly.

Also within the loop, a check is made on the state of the mouse buttons. If one (or more) has been pressed, then a CASE statement is used to determine the correct action. If the select button has been pressed (button value = 4) then the procedure has to switch between changing position and changing size. The pointer also has to be moved from one corner of the rectangle to the opposite one.

The rectangle is drawn near the start of the loop, and erased near the end, so that it remains visible for the maximum length of time within each cycle. Note the use of WAIT at line 1170 to synchronise deletion and redrawing of the rectangle with the vertical sync, and also the REPEAT...UNTIL loop at line 1150 which ensures that the mouse buttons return to a zero state after being pressed, and only after being pressed, before the loop is repeated. Even with the speed of the Archimedes, correct timing and synchronisation are just as important within such routines. The same problems of flickering images can occur just as easily as before, but more rapidly.

Examination of the coding in the rest of the procedure should clear up any further queries, as all is quite straightforward. A procedure such as this can be quite useful in an art or graphics package. For example, it allows the user to define any part of an existing display and then copy this elsewhere, or even produce stunning effects by 'drawing' with this image (see listing 9.1). It also allows any part of a screen display to be defined for saving as a sprite.

Listing 10.1 Dynamic mouse rectangle program

```
   10 REM >Chapter10-1
  100 MODE12:OFF
  120 p=320:q=256:r=160:s=128
  130 FROCrectangle(4,p,q,r,s!
  140 PRINT"x = ";p"
 1000 DEF PROCrectangle(colour,RETURN x1,RETURN y1,RETURN w,RETURN n)
 1010 LOCAL exit%,switcht,x,y:GCOL 3,colour
 1020 *POINTER
 1030 exit%=FALSE:switch%=TRUE
 1040 MOUSE TO x1,y1
 1060 REPEAT
 1070 RECTANGLE x1,y1,w,h
 1080 MOUSE x,y,z
```

```
1090 IF z THEN
1100 CASE z OF
1110 WHEN 4:switch%=NOT switch%
1120 IF switch% THEN MOUSE TO xl,yl ELSE MOUSE TO x+w,y+h
1130 WHEN 1:exit%=TRUE
1140 ENDCASE
1150 REPEAT:MOUSE x,y,z:UNTIL z=0
1160 ENDIF
1170 WAIT
1180 RECTANGLE xl,yl,w,h
1190 IF switch% THEN xl=x:yl=y ELSE w=x-xl:h=y-yl
1200 UNTIL exit%
1210 *POINTER 0
1220 ENDPROC
```

BASIC V For the Acorn Archimedes

11 : Sound

The Archimedes is provided with a sophisticated stereo sound system with up to eight voices or channels. The sound system is controlled by a number of modules which form part of the Arthur Operating System and RISC OS. BASIC V provides a number of instructions for controlling sound, including the sound command which provides some compatibility with previous versions of BBC BASIC.

Full control of the sound system is really only possible by directly using the SWI, or Operating System, calls provided for this purpose. A detailed description of these SWI calls is really beyond the scope of this book, but a number of these are accessible via star commands, and these are detailed below along with the instructions in BASIC for controlling sound.

BASIC Sound Instructions

Almost the simplest sound instructions must be SOUND ON and SOUND OFF, which may be used at any time to turn the Archimedes' whole sound system on or off. You can easily check this by pressing CTRL-G or typing VDU7, both of which make the computer 'beep'. Once SOUND OFF has been executed no beep will be heard until SOUND ON switches the sound system back on again.

The sound system uses up to eight voices, the number active at any time being set with the VOICES command. The number of voices must be a power of two - any other number is rounded up to the next value in sequence (1, 2, 4, or 8). Acorn recommends that the number of active voices should always be kept to a minimum as sound places heavy demands upon any computer, even the Archimedes.

A star command is needed to assign a waveform, or instrument, to a channel. There is some confusion of terminology here for which we can thank Acorn. BASIC refers to voices and waveforms, while Arthur and RISC OS refers to channels and voices. As a result, even Acorn's own manuals need reading with some care. A waveform may be assigned to a channel in one of two ways, by index or by name.

A list of the nine default voices (or waveforms) may be obtained using the command *VOICES. This will list the voices by name and by index number as follows:

BASIC V For the Acorn Archimedes

1. WaveSynth-Beep
2. StringLib-Soft
3. StringLib-Pluck
4. StringLib-Steel
5. StringLib-Hard
6. Percussion-Soft
7. Percussion-Medium
8. Percussion-Snare
9. Percussion-Noise

If you try executing this command, you should also see a figure '1' to the left of the first voice, WaveSynth-Beep. This shows that that voice is currently assigned to channel 1. This is the Archimedes 'beep' which is always connected to channel 1.

Any of the default, or any other voices, can be assigned to a channel using the command:

```
*CHANNELVOICE <channel> <voice index/name>
```

Thus the beep could be given the voice 'Percussion-Soft' by writing:

```
*CHANNELVOICE 1 6
```

or:

```
*CHANNELVOICE 1 Percussion-Soft
```

Although longer, the second format is perhaps preferable, as using an index is dependent upon the order in which a set of voices is loaded. There is also an alternative BASIC keyword, VOICE, not documented in the original User Guide, which performs the same function in this case, so the last command above could also be written:

```
VOICE 1,"Percussion-Soft"
```

The second parameter is the name of a voice and, as with other BASIC instructions, should be either a string variable or expression, or enclosed in quotes as here. Try experimenting, using either method, by using other voices to become the 'beep' in turn.

Setting the Stereo Position

The stereo position of each channel may be specified with the STEREO instruction. The position is given as a number in the range -127 to +127, where -127 indicates the extreme left, and +127 the extreme right. For example:

```
STEREO 1,0
```

77

BASIC V For the Acorn Archimedes

would position channel 1 centrally, ie, mono reproduction. However, as indicated in the User Guide, there are only seven discrete positions. As a result you could use the following set of values to specify all the stereo positions:

```
-80, -48, -16, 0, +16, +48, +80
```

moving from left to right. The effect of this instruction will only be apparent on the sound output through the miniature stereo jack socket at the rear of the Archimedes.

Setting and Reading the Beat

The BEATS statement allows channels to be synchronised together. The beat counter counts from 0 to n-1 where n is the value specified in the beats statement. When the value of n is reached the beat counter resets itself to 0. The syntax is simply:

```
BEATS n
```

The keyword BEATS can also be used to return its current setting, for example by typing:

```
PRINT BEATS
```

There is a second very similar keyword, BEAT. The value of this pseudo-variable returns the current value of the beat counter, and will therefore be in the range 0 to n, where n is the value specified with the BEATS instruction.

The value specified in the BEATS statement can be used in conjunction with the SOUND instruction (see later) to fix the position of notes within a bar of music. BEAT can be used to ensure that sounds are correctly synchronised. An example will tie all this together shortly.

Setting and Reading the Tempo

The rate at which the beat counter is incremented is determined by the tempo. This is set with the TEMPO statement, and as with BEATS, TEMPO can set the corresponding rate, or return the value to which the tempo is currently set. Therefore:

```
TEMPO n
```

will set the tempo to n, while:

```
PRINT TEMPO
```

will print out the current setting of the tempo. The value of n should be

BASIC V For the Acorn Archimedes

thought of as a four digit hexadecimal number, starting with '&', where the three right-most digits are a fraction less than one. A rate of &1000, the default, represents a tempo of one beat per centi-second, whilst &2000 represents double that rate, and so on.

Sound Statement

To create a sound or note, you need to use the SOUND instruction. The format of this is:

```
SOUND <channel>, <amplitude>, <pitch>, <duration> [,after]
```

For compatibility, this follows the same format as on the BBC Micro and Master series except for the optional 'after' parameter. The 'channel' parameter specifies which sound channel to use, with a maximum value of 8, but within the range determined by the VOICES instruction.

The 'amplitude' parameter provides volume control with -15 being the loudest and 0 the quietest. The pitch number is related to the standard musical scale by the table given in the User Guide, while duration takes a value in the range 0 to 254 (255 being forever) to specify the duration of the note in twentieths of a second.

The sound source will depend upon the voice which has been assigned to the channel specified in the SOUND command. The 'after' parameter, which is not essential, is used to specify the number of beats to be executed before a sound is to be made audible. As such it may be used to define the position of each note within the bar.

The program in listing 11.1 draws various of these aspects together. This is no musical masterpiece, but does serve to show some of the essential elements. If you run this program you will find it repeatedly plays the first three notes of a well known tune. The program starts by setting the TEMPO and BEATS count, and the maximum number of active voices. The voices themselves, selected from the built-in set, are allocated to four different channels.

Listing 11.1 Simple tune playing program.

```
 10 REM >Chap11-1
100 TEMPO &1000
110 BEATS 200
120 VOICES 4
130 VOICE 1,"StringLib-Soft"
140 VOICE2,"StringLib-Pluck"
150 VOICE2,"StringLib-Steel"
```

79

BASIC V For the Acorn Archimedes

```
160 VOICE2,"Percussion-Medium"
170 REPEAT
180 REPEAT UNTIL BEAT=0
190 SOUND 1, -15, 69, 5, 50
200 SOUND 2, -15, 61, 5, 100
210 SOUND 3, -15, 53, 5, 150
220 SOUND 4, -15, 200, 5, 50
230 SOUND 4, -15, 200, 5, 100
240 SOUND 4, -15, 200, 5, 150
250 REPEAT UNTIL BEAT <> 0
260 UNTIL FALSE
270 END
```

The REPEAT at line 170 marks the start of the main loop in the program. The following REPEAT...UNTIL statement at line 180 serves to synchronise the start of the bar for all channels, and the subsequent SOUND statements specify the notes to be played, and with the 'after' parameter, their relative positions within a bar of music. Thus, if BEATS has been specified at 200, an 'after' parameter of 50 will ensure a note sounds a quarter of the way through a bar.

Lastly, the REPEAT...UNTIL at line 250 ensures that the end of the bar is reached before the whole process is repeated.

Star Commands

As previously stated, many of the finer points of music generation on the Archimedes are best, or only, handled through Operating System (SWI) calls. Some of these are also provided in the form of star commands, and these are detailed briefly below for completeness.

*AUDIO ON/OFF   This performs the same functions as BASIC's SOUND ON/OFF instruction, switching the whole sound system on or off.

*SPEAKER ON/OFF   This controls the internal speaker, but leaves the external stereo output unaffected.

*STEREO c,n   Like *AUDIO this has the same purpose, and the same parameters, as the equivalent basic instruction.

*VOLUME n   This provides a volume control for the sound system where the value of 'n' may range from 1 (low volume) to 127 (high volume).

*SOUND c, a, p, d   Again, this is exactly the same as the SOUND statement in BASIC except that the additional 'after' parameter is not permitted.

*TEMPO n   Once more, a duplication of the similarly named BASIC instruction.

*QSOUND c, a, p, d, b   This command is the same as "SOUND but this time includes the additional 'after' parameter.

Sound is a highly complex subject, and anyone wishing to pursue it seriously and write their own programs will need to refer to the detailed section in the Programmer's Reference Manual. Be prepared for some machine code programming, or at the very least to handle a multitude of appropriate SWi calls to achieve the sophisticated sound output of which the Archimedes is capable. If you just want to use the sound system, then the Music Editor (Maestro) included on Acorn's Welcome disc should serve the purpose adequately.

BASIC V For the Acorn Archimedes

12 : Commands

BBC BASIC, like many interpreters, has always included a number of commands within its syntax, such as RUN and SAVE. Such commands are indistinguishable from basic instructions, being written solely in upper case. The difference is more one of user perception. Generally speaking, such commands apply to the program as a whole, such as the two examples given, or in some way control or change the environment containing the program. EDIT, for example, completely changes the context of a program. In practice, many of these so-called commands may also be included as part of a program. run, mistakenly in my view, is quite often included in this way.

BASIC V provides a number of additional commands compared with previous versions of BBC BASIC, and a number of others have been changed or extended in their function. These commands are as follows.

APPEND — This command may be used to append any saved file to another program already in memory. The file name may be given explicitly as a string in quotes, for example, append "Functions", or contained in a specified string variable such as append Prog$. If the specified file contains a basic program in tokenised format, then the line numbers and any references to them in the appended program will be renumbered to fo low the last line of the program already in memory. This is much better than the previous use of "SPOOL and *exec to achieve the same result, though these two commands may still have a part to play on occasion.

EDIT — In BASIC V, the edit command calls the arm basic Editor with the current program loaded, ready for editing. Shift-f4 returns from the editor back to basic. The editor is described in the User Guide and provides an easy-to-use facility for basic programmers.

HELP — This command by itself gives information about the current BASIC program, such as size in bytes. The command 'HELP' displays all BASIC keywords, while HELP followed by an initial letter gives all keywords beginning with that letter. HELP followed by an individual keyword gives a description of that keyword.

LVAR — When developing or debugging a program this command can be useful, as it displays the current state of all the inbuilt integer variables and all other variables used in your

BASIC V For the Acorn Archimedes

program. It also lists the procedures and functions called by the program, indicating the type of each parameter, real, integer or string, and the first lines of any loaded procedure and function libraries (see Chapter Five). It also lists arrays together with their dimensioned size. The limitation in the use of lvar which, in some circumstances, could be to your advantage, is that only those variables, procedures and functions referenced prior to the lvar call will be listed. So, for example, only those procedures and functions which have been called will appear, not necessarily all the procedures and functions defined in a program.

SAVE If the first line of a program consists of a rem statement followed by '>', then the save command, without any further specification, will save the current BASIC program under the file name specified after the '>'. For example, starting a program with:

```
10 REM >Graphl
```

would result in the save command saving the program using the name Graphl. This is a most useful facility. Editing the file name as program development progresses enables different versions to be named and saved quite easily. Note that no warning is given if this use of the save command overwrites an existing file with the same name.

LISTO The listo command now works as follows, depending on the number following the command:

0	no changes
bit 0 =1	a single space after the line number
bit 1 =1	indent any structures
bit 2 =1	split when':' encountered
bit 3 =1	don't list line numbers
bit 4 =1	list tokens in lower case

TWIN Calls the Twin text editor to edit the current basic program.

TWIN0 Calls the Twin text editor with a listo capability, ie. the TWIN0 command should be followed by a number as defined for LISTO.

TRACE The trace command has been enhanced to trace procedures and functions, and to trace in single-step mode. Various single parameters may follow the trace command as detailed below:

```
TRACE <expression>
```

83

BASIC V For the Acorn Archimedes

will display all line numbers encountered below (that is after) the value of <expression>.

```
TRACE ON
```

will trace all line numbers, and is thus equivalent to trace 65279, the highest possible line number.

```
TRACE PROC
```

will display the name of each procedure or function encountered

```
TRACE STEP <expression>
TRACE STEP ON
TRACE STEP PROC
```

are similar to the first three variations on trace described above except that when a line number, or procedure or function name, has been displayed, execution of the program in question pauses until a key is pressed.

```
TRACE OFF
```

simply switches the trace facility off. The trace command can be included anywhere within a program, and is a useful aid for resolving some of the knottier problems which may occur during program development.

13 : ARM Assembler

Although this book is not concerned with programming in arm assembler as such, it is appropriate to look at how assembler may be incorporated into BASIC programs, and how assembled routines may be called. BBC BASIC has always included a full assembler as part of its facilities, so we shall concentrate on the changes that have come about through the use of ARM assembler (instead of the 6502 assembler of earlier BBC Micros), and its incorporation into BASIC V.

Embedding ARM assembly language code in a BASIC program follows the same pattern as before. An area of memory must be defined for the assembled code using the dim statement. The assembly code is enclosed in square brackets, normally in a FOR...NEXT loop which makes two passes through the code. The typical outline of this is shown below:

```
DIM code_area% 400
FOR pass%=0 TO 3 STEP 3
P%==code_area%
[
OPT pass%
]
NEXT pass%
```

In addition to the use of P% to act as a program counter during assembly, the variable O% can additionally be used so that the code is assembled to run from an address different to that at which the code is being assembled. In that case, P% is set to the address that the code will be run from, and O% is set to the address at which the code will be (temporarily) assembled. This all follows exactly the same format as in previous versions of BBC BASIC.

If the machine code routine is to be called from BASIC, and a return made back to basic, then the address stored in register R14 should always be used to return to BASIC. Typically this would be effected by specifying MOV PC,Rl4 as the last executable instruction.

BASIC V also provides a number of assembler directives, but because we are now dealing with ARM rather than 6502 assembler, there are some differences compared with those used previously. Of course, their functions are broadly the same as before, the facility to insert specified values, characters and strings as part of the assembled code. The directives now available are as follows:

EQUB <int>   Define one byte of memory from the LSB (least significant byte) of the integer value 'int.

BASIC V For the Acorn Archimedes

EQUW <int>	Define two bytes of memory from 'int'
EQUD <int>	Define four bytes of memory from 'int'
EQUS <string>	Load between 0 and 256 bytes of memory with the given string.
ALIGN	Align the values of P% (and O%) to the next word boundary.
ADR <reg>,<addr>	Assemble an instruction to load the specified address into the given register (R0 to Rl5) in position independent format.

The first four directives have alternative mnemonics (DCB, DCW, DCD, and DCS respectively) which may be used in place of those given above. These directives are very similar to their 6502 equivalents. The values or strings specified may be expressions. The ALIGN directive is used, after EQUS for example, to ensure that the next instruction starts on a word boundary.

The Archimedes is a 32-bit (four bytes) machine, compared to the 8 bits of the 6502. This can be quite important.

The ADR directive looks very much like an ARM assembler mnemonic, but this is not the case. Its purpose is to generate an assembled instruction as part of the resulting machine code program which, when executed, will cause the address specified in the directive to be loaded into a particular register. The address is in position independent format, which means that it is specified as an offset from the current value of the pc (program counter). Thus:

```
ADR R0,data
```

will load the address at which 'data' is assembled into R0.

```
LDR R0,data
```

will load the value at address 'data' into R0.

All of the above information is covered in some detail in Part Two of the Programmer's Reference Manual.

Calling Machine Code Routines

BASIC programs can call machine code routines by using USR or CALL, much as with earlier versions of BBC BASIC. USR is the simplest by far of these two calls. It is effectively a function whose only parameter is the start address of the machine code routine being called, and which returns the value left in the first register, R0. No parameters other than the address of the routine itself are allowed.

BASIC V For the Acorn Archimedes

The call instruction is more comprehensive, allowing parameters as well as the start address to be specified. The parameters are accessed through a parameter block which must be set up by the BASIC program before executing CALL. On entry to the machine code routine, the registers are set up as follows:

Register	Set up as
R0-R7	Values of built-in integers A% - H%
R8	Pointer to basic's workspace (start address referred to as argp)
R9	Pointer to a list of L-values of the parameters
R10	Number of parameters
R11	Pointer to basic's string accumulator
R12	Pointer to current basic statement
R13	Pointer to basic's stack
R14	Return address for BASIC

On the Archimedes, up to eight values may be passed to the first eight registers (ro to R7) by assigning them to the appropriate integer variables. This is equally valid for routines which are accessed with USR. This means there are two ways of passing values to a machine code routine which is CALLed. Using A% to H% is certainly an easy way of entering initial values into any of the registers R0 to R7 for routines called by either USR or CALL.

Variables that are specified as parameters following CALL can be used to both supply values to the machine code routine, and as a means for the routine to return values. Note too, that if the routine called was to change the values of any variables passed as parameters, then these will retain their new values on a return to BASIC.

Writing machine code routines is a book in itself, and unravelling the parameters and other information can be quite a complex and daunting task. The following sections deal with what is involved, but unless you are familiar with parameter passing, on the 6502-based BBC micro for example, you may well wish to skip the rest of this chapter.

For a simple approach, use A% to H% to pass values to a routine. To return values, use indirection operators to access memory locations defined within the assembler routine to which the results have been assigned. The following, very simple, example adds together the contents of ro and Ri (A% and B% in the calling program), and leaves the result at the address 'result'.

```
.start
ADD R2,RG,R1
STR R2,result
MOV PC,R14
```

BASIC V For the Acorn Archimedes

```
.result
EQUD 0
```

If this were embedded in a BASIC program, and assembled as explained previously, it could then be called as in the following example:

```
A%=123
B%=456
CALL start
PRINT [result
```

Several results could be left in a table starting at 'result', and then accessed as:

```
PRINT [result
PRINT result! 4
PRINT result'8
```

and so on. Of course, if a routine is only going to return a single value, it may be best to assign this to R0 and use the USR function which returns the contents of this register. The routine above could have been written:

```
.start
ADD R0,R0,R1
MOV PC,R14
```

and called by typing:

```
A%=123
B%=456
PRINT USR(start)
```

Using CALL with Parameter Passing.

We will now examine the details of parameter passing using the CALL statement. This is also covered in the User Guide, under the keyword CALL, in some detail, but this manual gives virtually no other information on arm assembler at all. You will need to refer to the Programmer's Reference Manual, or to any of the books on this subject, for more detailed information and guidance.

Refer once again to the table showing the settings of the 16 registers on entry. The L-value of a variable is the address in memory at which the value is stored. R9 is a pointer to a table, held in reverse order, consisting of two words for each parameter passed, its L-value and its type. The range of possible types is listed below.

BASIC V For the Acorn Archimedes

BASIC	Type	Address points to	Comment
?name	0	byte-aligned byte	byte value
!name	4	byte-aligned word	four-byte integer
name%	4	word-aligned word	four-byte integer
name%(n)	4	word-aligned word	integer array element
|name	5	byte-aligned 5 bytes	five-byte real
name	5	byte-aligned 5 bytes	five-byte real
name(n)	5	byte-aligned 5 bytes	real array element
name$	128	byte-aligned 5 bytes	address (4 bytes) and length (1 byte) of string
name$(n)	128	byte-aligned 5 bytes	address (4 bytes) and length (1 byte) of string array element
$name	129	byte-aligned bytes	string terminated by ASCII 13
name%()	256+4	word-aligned word	pointer to integer array
name()	256+5	word-aligned word	pointer to real array
name$()	256+128	word-aligned word	pointer to string array

For each variable passed as a parameter, the table shows the type number and the information pointed to by the associated address. Any of the data types recognised by BASIC, from a single byte to a whole array, may be passed as a parameter. For whole arrays, the address provides a pointer to a list of all the values needed to access the array from within the called machine code routine. If the array has not previously been dimensioned, the pointer (word-aligned word) contains zero. Otherwise, the list of words pointed to by the word pointer is as follows:

```
word+0      first dimension limit (+1)
word+4      2nd dimension limit (+1)
........
word+n      0
word+n+4    total number of entries in array
word+n+8    the zero element of the array
```

The dimension limits are the limits to which the array was dimensioned in a DIM statement, with 1 added in each case. The list of limits is terminated by a zero word. The following two words contain the total number of possible entries in the array, and the value of the first (position 0) element.

Register R14 contains the address of a branch instruction to return to BASIC. The last instruction in a machine code routine, MOV PC,R14, copies that

BASIC V For the Acorn Archimedes

address to the PC, which causes the branch instruction to be executed to effect the return. The words following that specified in R14 contain various values relating to the current BASIC program as follows. Each word is an offset from ARGP whose location is stored in R8.

Register	Set up as
RI4	return address to BASIC
R14+4	string accumulator
R14+8	current value of PAGE
R14+12	current value of TOP
R14+16	current value of LOMEM (start of BASIC variable table)
R14+20	current value of HIMEM (BASIC end of stack)
RI4+24	limit of available memory (MEMLIMIT)
R14+28	start of free space
R14+32	current value of COUNT
R14+36	not used
R14+40	exception flag (contains byte-aligned bytes)
R14+44	current value of WIDTH

Locations from R14+48 onwards contain the addresses of a set of internal routines as follows.

VARIND	returns the value and type of a parameter
STOREA	converts between formats, eg, integer and real
STSTORE	store a string
LVBLNK	obtain address and type of variable for VARIND
CREATE	create a variable if LVBLNK fails
EXPR	evaluates an expression supplied as a string
MATCH	analyse source string lexically
TOKENADDR	returns a string corresponding to a given token

We have been getting into progressively deeper waters here, and are now well and truly into the realms of the machine code programmer. We will therefore call a halt, and refer the reader to the *Programmer's Reference Manual* and other books on this subject for more information.

14 : Operating System Calls

The Archimedes Operating Systems, Arthur and RISC OS, provide a wealth of routines that may be called by the user program, even from within BASIC. In fact, the only way to exploit the full potential of the machine is by making use of these detailed routines. Some Operating System functions are packaged up in BASIC for convenience, such as the VDU calls and the PLOT commands. Further functions are available in the form of star commands, though for greater flexibility these are often called from within basic programs using the OSCLI call.

However, to make full use of all the system functions available, they must be called more directly. Previous versions of BBC basic relied on the use of CALL (and sometimes USR) to access system functions, but BASIC V provides a new, general purpose call to do this. This is the SYS function, and it has its direct counterpart in ARM assembler in the form of the SWI call.

A SWI call is a SoftWare Interrupt. When a SWI call is executed, the ARM processor leaves the current program and jumps to a fixed location in memory. This in turn contains a branch instruction into the Operating System ROM where the SWI call is decoded and the correct routine entered, with appropriate parameters. Once execution of the call is complete, control is returned to the user's program.

Every legitimate SWI call has a number to identify it, but the name of the SWI can be used instead (it must be precisely specified including use of upper and lower case characters), and this is much to be preferred for readability. The name must be enclosed in inverted commas, as with any string. The SWI call also allows parameters to be passed to the routine called, and provides for information to be returned.

SYS Calls

In BASIC V, SYS is the exact counterpart of the SWI call, and should be used to access all Operating System routines. The general format of a SYS call is as follows:

    SYS <name/number>,<parameters> TO <variables> ;<flags>

Again, note that the name of the SYS call, the same name as for the corresponding SWI call, must be in inverted commas. Up to eight 'input' parameters may be specified immediately following the SYS call name or number, and these values are assigned, in order, to the first eight registers,

BASIC V For the Acorn Archimedes

R0 to R7. If a parameter supplies a numeric value, this is converted to integer format and stored in the corresponding register; if the parameter supplies a string, a zero byte is added to the end of the string, and the string stored on BASIC's stack at a word-aligned start address, and a pointer to the string placed in the appropriate register.

Following the keyword TO, a list of 'output' variables can be included, which will be used to return values to the calling program. These operate as the counterpart of the input parameters, that is, each variable in turn is associated with the registers R0 to R7. If the variable is numeric, the value in the corresponding register is returned in the appropriate format, real or integer, to the variable. If the variable is of type string, the contents of the corresponding register are treated as a pointer to a string stored in memory, and this string is then assigned to the string variable.

The first parameter is separated from the SYS function name by a comma, and subsequent parameters are separated from each other by further commas. For the output variables, the first is separated from the 'TO' by a space, the remainder by commas. Both parameters and variables in sequence may be omitted provided the commas are included. Therefore:

```
SYS "DummyFunction",,b,c,,e TO A,,,,E
```

would result in the input values supplied by b, c, and e being linked to registers Ri, R2 and R4, with the output variables A and E being linked to registers R0 and R4. Notice, on the input side, the comma immediately following the SYS function name indicating that the value which would be linked to register ro has been omitted. By this means, any of the registers R0 to R7 can be linked to input parameters or output variables as required, even if intermediate registers are not used. Depending on how some SYS functions are used, you may find that you use different register combinations in different contexts with the same sys call. Some more examples of sys call syntax are given at the end of this chapter.

The same variables may be included on both the input and output sides of the SYS call, and will result in the input parameters being overwritten. The only point to watch, if this is followed, is that a return string cannot exceed the length of an input string where the same variable is to be used for both.

You will find, in practice, that some SYS calls need no parameters at all, some need input parameters, some output parameters and some both. In addition, if a variable is specified following a semi-colon at the end of a SYS call, this will be set to the processor flag bits on return. These are the bits NZCV from the arm status register. The input parameters may be values or expressions, including simple variables, but the output parameters, because they are used to return values, must always be specified as variables.

BASIC V For the Acorn Archimedes

Three particular SWI, or SYS, calls are worth mentioning individually. The call OS_CLI is directly equivalent to OSCLI, and passes a string to the Command Line Interpreter. The calls OS_Byte and OS_Word each provide a variety of different functions, and are provided in this form for the sake of compatibility with similarly named calls on the BBC Micro and Master series.

All the SWI calls are documented in the Programmer's Reference Manual, and this is essential reading if you want to take full advantage of them. Remember also that some SWI calls directly reference routines in the Operating System ROM, while others call routines in relocatable modules. In practice the two are indistinguishable, and all such calls can be thought of as system calls.

As an indication of what can be achieved, I have listed some of the SWI calls below.

OS_Byte,13	Disable event
OS_Byte,14	Enable event
OS_GenerateEvent	Generate an event
OS_SpriteOp	General sprite call providing more options than star commands alone
OS_ReadPalette	Read red, green, blue values for given logical colour
Wimp_Initialise	Initialise Wimp manager
Wimp_CreateWindow	Creates a window
Wimp_CreateIcon	Creates an icon
Wimp_DeleteWindow	Deletes a window definition
Wimp_OpenWindow	Display window on screen
Wimp_Poll	Check for any changes to windows

There are many more SYS calls to the Wimp manager.

Font_FindFont	Get pointer to a font
Font_LoseFont	Remove font definition

Again there are many more SYS calls to the Font manager and also to the sound scheduler.

Finally, I have included a number of SYS calls taken from working programs to show how they might appear within a program.

```
SYS "Wimp_OpenWindow",,offset
SYS "Wimp_CreateWindow",,block% TO handle
SYS "Sound_QSchedule",Beats%,&F0401C6,A%
```

BASIC V For the Acorn Archimedes

```
SYS "Sound_InstallVoice" TO ,NVoices%
SYS "OS_File",5,F$ TO F%,,,,C%,A%
SYS "OS_ReadPalette",pixel,16 TO ,,foreground,background
```

Notice the ways in which commas have been used in the above examples to select which registers are to be used for parameter passing.

15 : Miscellaneous Changes

This chapter contains a miscellaneous collection of bits and pieces of information related to BASIC V and its differences from previous versions of BBC BASIC, which could not readily be fitted into any of the previous chapters. If you cannot find what you are looking for elsewhere in this book, then you will probably find it here.

LINE INPUT

The statement line input is entirely equivalent to the existing INPUT LINE. If the input variable is of type string then all the user's input up to, but not including, Return will be assigned to that variable. If the input variable is numeric, then only a single value will be taken from the input stream.

ON and OFF

In the past, several different versions of VDU23 calls were discovered for switching the flashing cursor on and off. Later, with the advent of the Master and Compact, these calls gained respectable legitimacy. BASIC V has taken this process one stage further by providing simple keywords, ON and OFF, to perform this essential function. However, the OFF action is not permanent. As well as reappearing when a mode change takes place, cursor editing will also restore the flashing cursor to the screen.

QUIT

To leave basic and interact with RISC OS directly, use QUIT. Incidentally, to return to BASIC the abbreviation 'B.' will no longer suffice, at least 'BA.' is now needed. Quitting to go to the system can sometimes prove useful. For example, if you attempt to load a relocatable module from within BASIC, you may encounter the message "Insufficient RMA space", but if the RMLoad command is executed from the system the problem is unlikely to arise as, in that context, the configured RMA space limit is ignored.

END

This keyword now has a second purpose, and may be used as a function to return the address of the limit of memory used by a program and its variables. BASIC always maintained this information in a zero page location, but it is now available through END rather than by dubious peeking at the appropriate location.

Mode Changes in Functions and Procedures

Mode changes can now be included in procedure and function definitions without any problems.

Improved PRINT Accuracy

The accuracy has now been improved when using PRINT and STR$ with numbers. For example, 0.05 now prints as 0.05 and not as 5E-2 as was previously the case.

Increased Line Number Range

The maximum line number for BASIC programs has been increased from 32767 to 65279 to cater better for larger programs. In memory, a program now terminates explicitly with two bytes, &0D &FF, whereas any byte with the top bit set would have marked the end of a program previously. Some program binary images created on earlier BBC micros may generate a "Bad program" error when loaded. This can be corrected by using *LOAD and locating and correcting the final byte. This is most unlikely to be a problem for the majority of programs.

Improved COUNT

Tabulation has been improved by using a 32-bit value for COUNT. This function keeps track of the current position within a line of text displayed or printed out.

Printed in Dunstable, United Kingdom